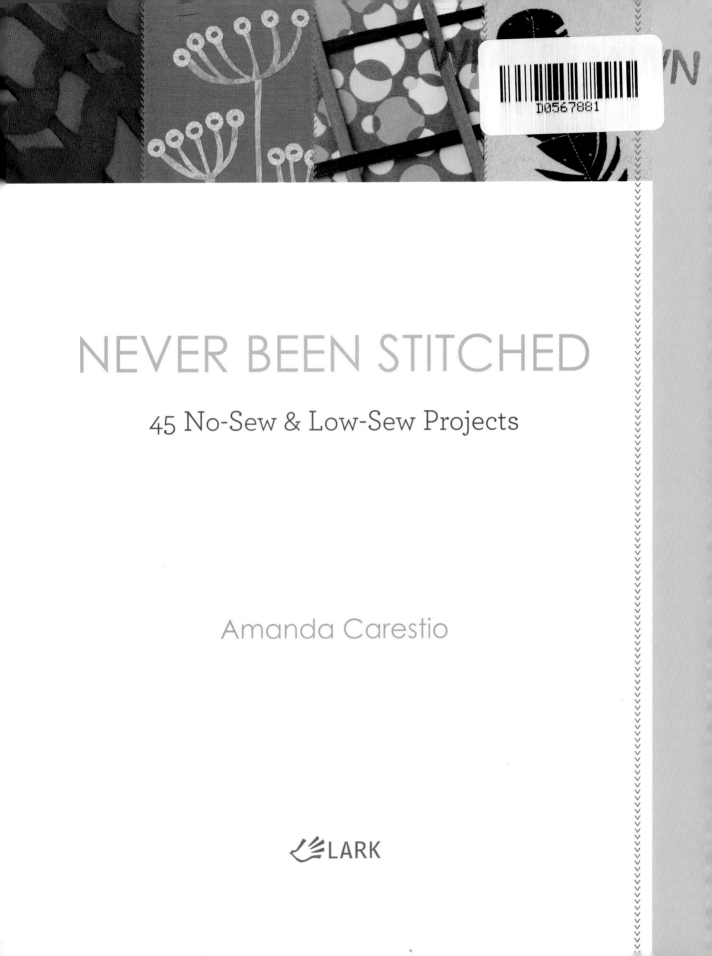

D0567881

NEVER BEEN STITCHED

45 No-Sew & Low-Sew Projects

Amanda Carestio

LARK

LARK

An Imprint of Sterling Publishing
387 Park Avenue South
New York, NY 10016

© 2014 by Lark Crafts, an Imprint of Sterling Publishing Co., Inc.

All rights reserved. No part of this publication may be reproduced, stored in a retrieval system, or transmitted, in any form or by any means, electronic, mechanical, photocopying, recording, or otherwise, without prior written permission from the publisher.

ISBN 978-1-4547-0421-8

Library of Congress Cataloging-in-Publication Data

Carestio, Amanda.
  Never been stitched : 45 no-sew and low-sew projects / Amanda Carestio.
    pages cm
  ISBN 978-1-4547-0421-8
  1. Textile crafts. 2. Handicraft. 3. Fusible materials in sewing. I. Title.
  TT699.C37 2013
  745.5--dc23

                      2013014105

Distributed in Canada by Sterling Publishing
c/o Canadian Manda Group, 165 Dufferin Street
Toronto, Ontario, Canada M6K 3H6
Distributed in the United Kingdom by GMC Distribution Services
Castle Place, 166 High Street, Lewes, East Sussex, England BN7 1XU
Distributed in Australia by Capricorn Link (Australia) Pty. Ltd.
P.O. Box 704, Windsor, NSW 2756, Australia

For information about custom editions, special sales, and premium and corporate purchases, please contact Sterling Special Sales at 800-805-5489 or specialsales@sterlingpublishing.com.

Email academic@larkbooks.com for information about desk and examination copies. The complete policy can be found at larkcrafts.com.

Every effort has been made to ensure that all the information in this book is accurate. However, due to differing conditions, tools, and individual skills, the publisher cannot be responsible for any injuries, losses, and other damages that may result from the use of the information in this book.

Manufactured in China

2 4 6 8 10 9 7 5 3 1

larkcrafts.com

CONTENTS

>>>

THE PROJECTS

Why NOT stitch these projects today? Because you don't have to!

Hi, friends. And welcome to *Never Been Stitched*. I invite you to take a break from your sewing machine, explore a different section of the craft store, and discover the pure joy of wrapping, tying, and gluing your way to crafty bliss....all while keeping your well-established fabric addiction intact. Or maybe you're a craft fanatic who's into handmade but never mastered threading your sewing machine? Relax: there's plenty you can do with fabric that doesn't involve a presser foot.

I've assembled a set of 45 fabulous things (from equally fabulous designers) to make for kids, for the home, for you to wear and accessorize with, or for gifts, all sans the stitching. Or sometimes with just a little stitching. With just a few simple steps, you can:

Wear... a woven chevron cowl made with fleece and only a single seam (page 28).

Decorate... your space with a stunning decoupaged hexagon art panel (page 36).

Play... with a clever caterpillar friend made from a repurposed jersey pillowcase (page 90).

Carry... all your belongings in a fashionable tote made from an upcycled t-shirt (page 97).

Give... a set of wee felt journals perfect for jotting notes (page 113).

Let the icons guide you on your no-sew/low-sew adventure. Here's a handy guide:

NO SEW	LOW SEW
This project involves absolutely no sewing. Zip, zero, nada.	This project calls for some simple sewing, from a tiny bit (a decorative stitch, a button) to one, two, or more simple seams.

Keep in mind that with no-sew projects, you always have the option to add stitched details or to sew elements together instead. With low-sew, you also have options. I've included Skip The Stitching ideas along the way, so if a pattern calls for stitching but you don't feel inclined, you don't have to. The projects that involve sewing can often be stitched by hand, though a sewing machine is handy for some.

For each project, you'll also get a quick list of what main techniques are involved. From cutting to knotting to fusing and beyond, there's nothing too complicated here. Which also means these projects make great last-minute gifts and are perfect for little crafters.

So pick a project, gather what you need, and get started. But whatever you do, just don't stitch it!

GETTING STARTED

>>>

The absolute beauty of these no-sew and low-sew projects is that you don't need much to get started. Grab an old t-shirt, some pins, and a pair of sharp scissors...and you're ready to get your make on!

MATERIALS

The raw materials used in this book run the (quite fabulous!) gamut from fresh-off-the-bolt jersey to repurposed t-shirts to grommets, glue...and beyond.

Fabric

A few of the projects in this book might require you to purchase new fabric, which I'm sure is highly disappointing. When you're in the store and you're thinking no-/low-sew, look for fabrics with a raw edge that doesn't ravel, like the following:

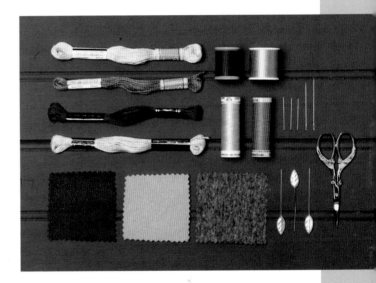

- felt
- fleece
- vinyl
- oilcloth
- ribbon or strapping
- jersey and knits
- or anything that doesn't require you to finish the edges.

A good number of projects take advantage of "fabric" with edges that are already finished, which means less sewing for you: placemats, bandanas, ribbon, or found crewel panels you picked up at a thrift store (because who can help but collect those pretty things?). When in doubt, you can also take premade items like tote bags and pillowcases apart for "fabric" and then totally transform them. Fabric scraps are also put to good use here. Even with raw edges, scraps are particularly lovely for appliqué techniques.

One of my favorite kinds of no-sew projects involves taking something old and making it new again with embellishments. With just a few scraps of fabric and easy appliqué, you can completely update an old garment for next season.

Other Supplies

Don't stop at the fabric section! Many of the projects in this book incorporate fiberfill or stuffing, paper, wood, grommets, and more, all available at your average craft or home improvement store...maybe just in a different section than you're used to.

5

And for this book, we've embraced fabric glue...and we're not apologizing. Gather up a host of other sticky stuff fusible web tape (also called hem tape), like fusible webbing sheets, and fray retardant, and you'll be set for most no-sew bonding scenarios.

TOOLS

Because these projects are no- and low-sew, you might need a few tools outside of your standard sewing supplies. What you'll need for each project will vary depending on the type of technique used, but here are a few simple items you'll want to have on hand to make the projects in this book: scissors, fabric marker,

pencil, ruler, pins, iron and ironing board, a sewing needle, and thread. A sewing machine is not an absolute necessity, though for some projects, it will make things go a bit faster.

You might also need the occasional hammer (for grommets), a staple gun for a project or two, or a paint brush (for glue), again depending on the project you're making.

TECHNIQUES

Low-tech, quick, and cool—that is music to my crafty ears. You don't need to know any fancy techniques to make the projects in this book.

No-sew Techniques

If you spend a lot of quality time with your sewing machine, take a break and try something different with these no-sew techniques.

Grommets: Besides making a hard-core fashion statement all their own, grommets are highly useful in no-sew situations. Plus, installing them is somewhat therapeutic. Simply trace your grommet onto your fabric, cut an "x" inside the circle, cut out the segments of the "x," place the grommet and washer in the hole on both sides of the fabric, and hammer away using the setter and backing block (these usually come in a pack with the grommets). Done!

Bonding, fusing, and gluing: If it's been awhile since you've played with decoupage, break out the Mod Podge® and rejoice! Simply lay or glue your elements onto your surface and brush or use a brayer to spread a layer of Mod Podge® on top.

6

Hem tape, seam binding, and fusible webbing (more on that later) are used in essentially the same way: iron the tape or webbing to your fabric, remove any paper backing, and iron to the other side or layer of fabric.

No need to over-think all the fabulous applications for fabric glue: the stuff is just amazing.

Braiding, tying, folding, and knotting: There's nothing more involved here than what is required to make your basic fourth-grade friendship bracelet. Simply follow the project instructions to manipulate your fabrics.

Low-sew Techniques

A seam here, a running stitch there, many of the projects in this book call for a little bit of sewing, but we've kept it simple. For most, you can hand-sew, but for others, a sewing machine will come in handy.

Hemming: If the fabric you're using doesn't come with a pre-finished edge or ravels easily, you'll want to hem the edges. Simple fold and press the edge under twice (per the pattern instructions), and sew along the edge. Easy enough! Even easier: skip the sewing and use hem tape instead.

Appliqué: Nothing fancy here: stitch or stick one layer of fabric on top of another. When it comes to this technique, fusible webbing–especially the paper backed kind–is your friend. A few magical steps and you've basically created your own iron-on. Simply trace your appliqué shape onto the paper side of the webbing, iron it to the back of your fabric, cut the shape out, remove the backing, and iron the shape in place where it needs to go. And with fusible web, you've got the option to skip the stitching altogether, especially if your item doesn't need to be washed or washed too often.

Simple embroidery: Created with embroidery floss and needle, sometimes a little hand-stitching can supply that handmade flavor to a project.

Using Templates

Starting on page 120, you'll find all the templates you need to make the projects in this book. Just enlarge the templates using the percentages listed, cut them out and pin them or trace them on your fabric, and cut out your fabric shapes.

And with that, you're on your way to no-sew and low-sew bliss! Enjoy!

AUTUMN LEAVES SKIRT

Grab a stack of fall-colored scraps and some fusible web, and update a favorite skirt with a simple border of appliquéd leaves.

Try this in spring colors.

DESIGNER:
Jenny Bartoy

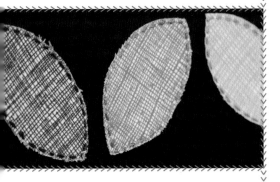

STITCH FACTOR:

low sew

>>>>>>>>>>>>>>

WHAT YOU'LL DO:
Fused appliqué & simple
sewing (optional)

You Will Need:

» Iron and ironing surface
» Fabric scraps in coordinating
  colors and prints for the leaves
» Paper-backed fusible web
» Template (page 120)
» Pencil or erasable pen
» Sharp scissors
» A plain skirt to embellish
» Embroidery needle and floss in
  coordinating colors (optional)
» Embroidery hoop (optional)

Cut the Scraps

1. Back the fabric scraps with the fusible web following the manufacturer's instructions.

2. Using the template and a pencil, trace and cut out 20 leaves from the prepped fabric scraps. Choose a balanced mix of colors and prints that evoke autumn.

TIP: *To prevent the fabric from fraying when you remove the paper backing, cut a rough square around each leaf shape, peel back the paper halfway, then carefully cut out the leaf.*

3. Press the skirt and lay the bottom edge flat on the ironing surface.

Arrange the Leaves

4. Starting with the front of the skirt, arrange your leaves in an order that is pleasing to your eye, using the photo as a guide. The bottom tips of the leaves should be 1 inch (2.5 cm) from the bottom hem of the skirt. There should be ¼ to ½ inch (6 mm to 1.3 cm) between the tips of adjoining leaves. If your skirt is wider and requires more leaves than the 20 you prepped, cut out more and continue the design until you reach the side seams.

5. Peel off the paper backing and fuse the leaves to the skirt, following the manufacturer's instructions. Repeat steps 4 and 5 for the back of the skirt.

Stitch the Shapes

6. Add detailing to the leaves by embroidering the edges with a basic running stitch in a coordinating floss color.

Skip the Stitching!
You don't have to embroider the leaves if you're okay with a little raveling. Simply fuse the leaves in place, and wash your skirt on a gentle cycle or by hand.

9

Wear

SIDE-TIED TUNIC

A sophisticated boat-neck, a bold stripe pattern, and flirty ties: this jersey tunic may become a new staple in your wardrobe.

DESIGNER:
Jessica Fediw

STITCH FACTOR:

no sew

>>>>>>>>>>>>>>

WHAT YOU'LL DO:
Knotting & cutting

figure 1

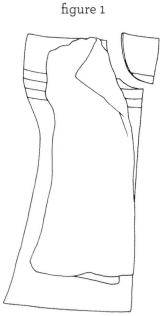

You Will Need:

» 1 yard (0.9 m) of knit fabric*
» A short-sleeved shirt that fits you well
» Sharp scissors
» Tape measure or ruler

*Note: *Make sure the fabric stretches along the length-wise grain; otherwise it won't work for this project. To see if the fabric stretches along the lengthwise grain, pull it sideways when it's on the bolt. If it stretches that way, then it will work.*

Cut the Shirt

1. Fold the knit fabric in half lengthwise (it will already be this way if it's right off the bolt). Fold it in half again, this time widthwise. You will have two sides where the fabric is folded and two sides where it will be open (raw edges).

2. Fold your shirt in half lengthwise, matching the sides, sleeves, and shoulders. Place the fold of the shirt on the side fold of the fabric, making sure the shoulders of the shirt are at the top fold of the fabric.

3. Cut a basic silhouette of the shirt from the knit fabric, including the neckline. Make sure to leave some extra room—about 1½ inch (3.8 cm)—on the side so there is room for the ties (figure 1).

continued ⟶

Wear

Create the Slits

4. Turn both edges of one side of the shirt in. Cut slits down the sides from underneath the armpit area to the bottom of the shirt about 1 to 2 inches (2.5 to 5.1 cm) apart (figure 2). Make sure they are small, as the material will stretch.

5. Repeat on the other side, making sure to cut slits in the same places for an even look.

Add the Ties

6. Use the leftover fabric to cut ties that measure 1½ x 10 inches (3.8 x 25.4 cm). Make the same number of ties as slits you cut in step 4.

7. Slip a tie through one of the slits, making sure to go through both sides of the shirt, then double-knot it in place. Repeat for the rest of the ties.

figure 2

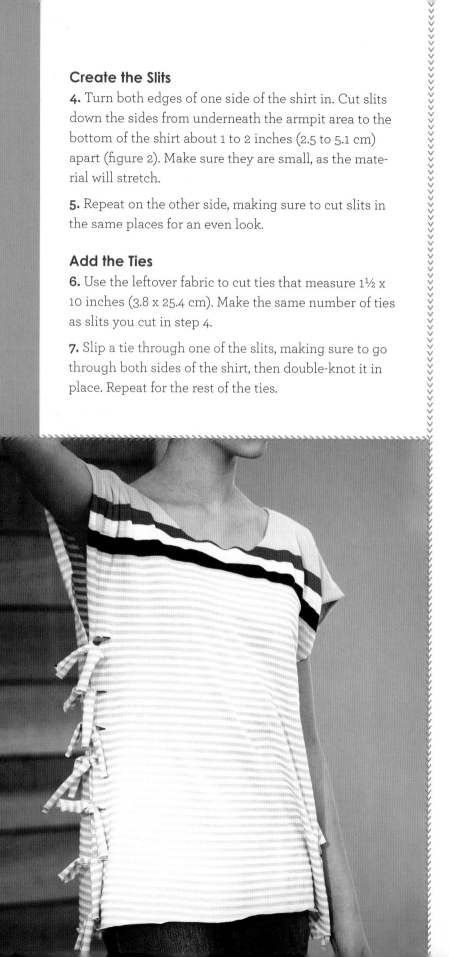

SHEER MAXI SKIRT

Go from sheer curtain to chic maxi with only a few simple stitches.
Wear your new (favorite!) skirt over leggings or a shorter skirt underneath.

From sheer
curtain to
stunning skirt!

DESIGNER: Yuka Yoneda, Clossette.com

STITCH FACTOR:

low sew

>>>>>>>>>>>>>>

WHAT YOU'LL DO:
Simple sewing

You Will Need:

» A long sheer or lace curtain in a color you like
» Straight pins
» A 1-inch (2.5 cm) piece of elastic in a color that complements the curtain color
» Sewing needle and thread that complements or matches the curtain color
» 1 large hook fastener

Prep the Skirt Panel

1. Wrap the curtain lengthwise around your waist as if you were going to tie a sarong. Since you're making a maxi-length skirt, you want the curtain to go almost all the way down to the floor if you want to wear the skirt with heels or slightly shorter than that if you plan to wear it with flats. If your curtain is too long, cut some of it off or hem it.

Create the Ruffle

2. To create the ruffle for the skirt, place a pin at the point where the fabric begins to overlap (while it's wrapped around your waist).

14

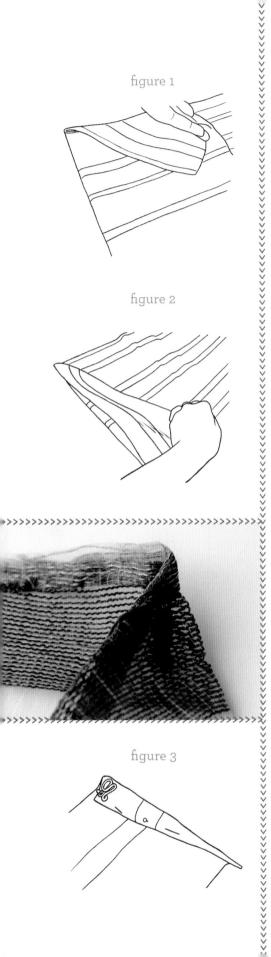

figure 1

figure 2

figure 3

3. Place the curtain wrong side up on a flat surface so that the pin is at the top. Starting where the pin is, fold the fabric inward perpendicularly.

4. Fold a skinny sliver of fabric down at about a 30° angle.

5. Fold downward again so that the edge of the skinny sliver of fabric meets the left folded edge of your curtain (figures 1 and 2). Once you have this sort of funnel-shaped ruffle, place some pins to keep it in place and try wrapping the curtain around your waist to see how it looks. Then make adjustments accordingly.

6. Once you have the ruffle exactly the way you want it and it's pinned down, lay the curtain right side up on the floor or another flat surface. Pin the 1-inch (2.5 cm) piece of elastic to the corner at the top of your ruffle. The elastic should be positioned vertically so that it's about halfway from either side of the ruffle edges.

7. Once you have your elastic in position, make five or six stitches at the top of it, make a knot, and cut the thread. Repeat for the bottom of the elastic.

Tip: *Since the curtain is sheer, make sure you knot the thread a few extra times to ensure that it will not pass through the fabric. For a clean-looking finish with no knots sticking out, make sure the first stitch enters from the side of the skirt that won't show when you're wearing it.*

Attach the Hook Fastener

8. Next, flip the curtain wrong side up and locate the corner of the skirt opposite the ruffle (where the hook should go so that it can attach to the elastic). To make the hook a bit more sturdy and secure, fold a little sliver of that corner down so you'll be sewing through two layers of material instead of just one. Then pin the hook in place (figure 3). Try to make it so that the hook is at least ½ inch (1.3 cm) away from the edge of your fabric so that it's nicely hidden when you wear your skirt.

9. Sew the hook in place.

15

FUN FRINGE SCARF

Everything is more fun with fringe! Simple tied fringe-ends turn a pair of old T-shirts into the perfect wear-with-anything scarf.

Favorite T-shirt revamp

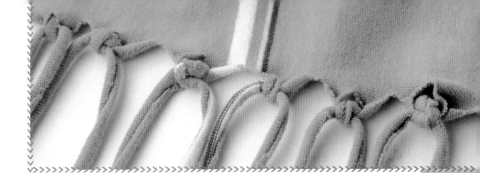

DESIGNER:
Cynthia Shaffer

STITCH FACTOR:

low sew

>>>>>>>>>>>>>

WHAT YOU'LL DO:
Cutting, simple
sewing & knotting

figure 1

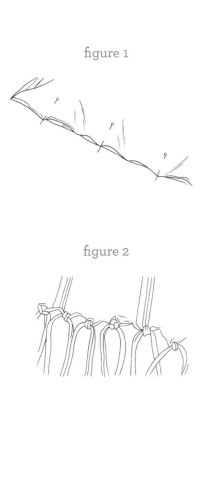

figure 2

You Will Need:

» Scissors
» 2 T-shirts in coordinating colors, size large
» Measuring tape or ruler
» Sewing machine or needle and thread
» Thread

Prep the Fabric

1. Cut the hems off of the 2 T-shirts.

2. Cut 15-inch (38.1 cm) strips from the body of the T-shirt.

3. Cut the sleeves off the T-shirts and cut the body portion into 15-inch (38.1 cm) widths.

4. Pin the short 15-inch (38.1 cm) edges together with right sides facing each other, and then stitch them using a ¼-inch (6 mm) seam allowance (figure 1).

5. Continue to stitch T-shirt lengths together until the scarf measures 76 inches (193 cm) long.

Create the Fringe

6. Lay the ends of the scarf flat and make 29 cuts up into the scarf, each 5 inches (12.7 cm) long and ½ inch (1.3 cm) wide, to create a fringe at both ends.

7. Using a square knot, tie two fringe strips together (figure 2) and then give them a bit of a tug to create a rolled rope effect. Repeat for the remaining fringe strips.

8. Knot the ends of the fringe.

17

JERSEY VEST

This jersey vest comes together without a single stitch. Wrap, fold, and tie the braided belt in different ways for multiple new looks.

DESIGNER:
Amanda Carestio

STITCH FACTOR:

no sew

>>>>>>>>>>>>>>

WHAT YOU'LL DO:
Cutting & braiding

figure 1

figure 2

figure 3

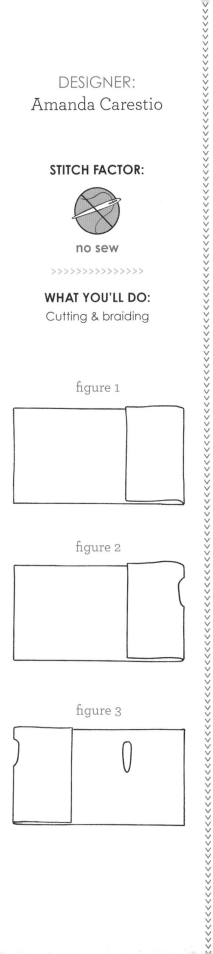

You Will Need:

» 2 yards (1.8 m) of jersey knit
   fabric, 60 inches (152.4 cm) wide
» Tape measure
» Scissors
» Template (page 120)

Make the Belt

1. With the fabric folded in half lengthwise with sel-vages together (as it is on the bolt), cut three 1½-inch (3.8 cm) strips off one end.

2. Knot the three strips together at one end, braid them, and knot the opposite end. Belt complete!

Cut the Vest

3. Measure across your shoulders, add 2 inches (5.1 cm), and multiply this number by three to get the length of fabric you'll need. For example, if your shoulders are 16 inches (40.6 cm) wide, add 2 inches (5.1 cm), and then multiply by three for a total of 54 inches (137.1 cm).

4. Cut the remaining fabric, still folded lengthwise, to the length measurement from step 3.

5. Fold one-third of the fabric over itself (figure 1).

6. Place the armhole template along the side folded edge 5 inches (12.7 cm) below the top folded edge (figure 2). Cut out the armhole.

7. Unfold the fabric and then fold one-third of the other end over itself (figure 3). Following step 6, cut out the other armhole.

8. Stick your arms through the armholes, tie the belt, and you're done!

BEADED TEE NECKLACE

I love the layered look, and this necklace delivers. Beaded strips of T-shirt jersey become chunky strands for this easy no-sew project.

DESIGNER:
Cynthia Shaffer

STITCH FACTOR:

no sew

>>>>>>>>>>>>>

WHAT YOU'LL DO:
Cutting & knotting

figure 1

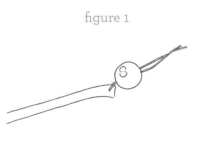

You Will Need:

» Rotary cutter and self-healing mat
» Ruler
» 1 navy blue T-shirt
» 1 maroon T-shirt
» 1 tan T-shirt
» Paper clip
» 26 wooden beads in three colors and in various sizes

Cut the Strips

1. Fold one of the T-shirts in half lengthwise and lay it flat on the cutting mat. Using the ruler and rotary cutter, cut off the hem.

2. Cut 1-inch (2.5 cm) crosswise strips from the body portion of the T-shirt.

3. Repeat steps 1 and 2 for the two remaining T-shirts.

Tip: *If the T-shirts have sewn side seams, then cut the bulk of the seam off the strips. If there is not a seam in the T-shirt, then cut the strips open.*

4. Give each strip a bit of a tug. The T-shirt strips will curl up into a rolled rope.

Add the Beads

5. Straighten the paper clip, then bend it in half to form a U shape.

6. Insert the paper clip into the end of one of the strips and then thread a bead onto the T-shirt strip (figure 1). Thread two or three beads at a time to give the necklace some variety.

7. Using a square knot, tie another T-shirt strip to this beaded strip. Cut the ends close to the knot.

8. Slide the bead down to the knot, and then tie another knot at the other end of the bead.

9. Tie the ends of the T-shirt strip together in a square knot to form a loop and cut the ends close to the knot.

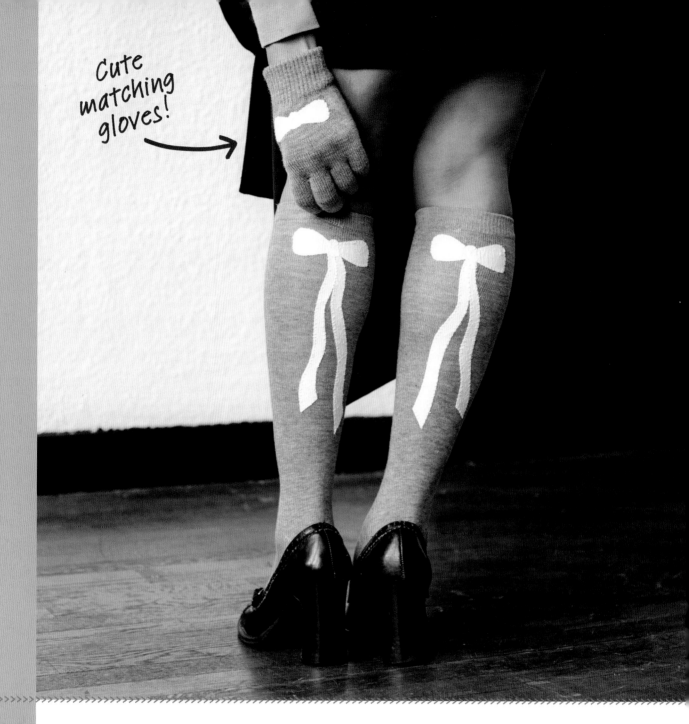

Cute matching gloves!

SWEET BOW SOCKS

Paired with a vintage dress or a flirty skirt, simple appliquéd bows make quite a fashion statement.

DESIGNER:
Cynthia Shaffer

STITCH FACTOR:

low sew

>>>>>>>>>>>>>

WHAT YOU'LL DO:
Fused appliqué
& simple sewing

figure 1

You Will Need:

» Piece of cardboard, 6½ x 11 inches (16.5 x 27.9 cm)
» 1 pair of light heather gray knee-high socks
» Straight pins
» Iron and ironing surface
» ¼ yard (22.9 cm) of paper-backed fusible web
» ¼ yard (22.9 cm) of white cotton fabric
» Templates A, B, and C (page 124)
» White perle cotton
» Large-eye hand-sewing needle

Find the Center

1. Cut a shape from the cardboard that measures 6½ inches (16.5 cm) at the top, 4 inches (10.2 cm) at the bottom, and 11 inches (27.9 cm) in length. Mark the center with a lengthwise dotted line.

2. With the sock folded in half, mark the center back of the sock with pins.

3. Slide the sock onto the cardboard shape, matching the pins with the center line.

Create the Appliques

4. Following the manufacturer's instructions, iron the fusible web onto the wrong side of the white cotton fabric.

5. Using Templates A, B, and C, trace two pairs of each–one normal and one reversed–onto the paper-backed fused fabric.

6. Cut out the traced shapes and peel off the paper backing.

7. Center the bow and tie pieces on the sock and fuse to the sock with an iron, following the manufacturer's instructions.

Attach the Bows & Ties

8. Using the white perle cotton and large-eye needle, overcast stitch around the bow and the ties (figure 1).

9. Repeat steps 7 and 8 for the second sock.

LACE-TRIMMED CARDIGAN

Update a basic cardigan with a bit of sweet, sophisticated lace.
Simply fuse lace scraps on the collar and the elbows.

DESIGNER:
Yuka Yoneda,
Clossette.com

STITCH FACTOR:

no sew

>>>>>>>>>>>>>>

WHAT YOU'LL DO:
Fused appliqué

You Will Need:

» An old crewneck cardigan
(or sweater)
» Iron and ironing surface
» Extra-strong paper-backed
fusible web
» A piece of lace, approxi-
mately 7 x 10 inches
(17.8 x 25.4 cm)
» Templates (page 120)
» Pencil
» Sharp scissors

Prep the Sweater
1. Wash, dry, and iron your cardigan.

Create the Appliqués
2. Cut two 3½-inch (8.9 cm) squares of paper-backed fusible web and two 3½-inch (8.9 cm) squares of lace.

3. Set the iron to the silk setting. When it is heated, place one of the fusible squares onto the ironing board, paper side down, and place a lace square on top of it. Set the hot iron on top of the squares for about 2 to 3 seconds and then remove. Check to see whether or not the squares have adhered together, and if not, carefully iron them a few more times until they do. Repeat this step with the other pair of squares.

4. When the adhered squares have cooled, use a pencil to trace the heart template on the paper side and cut the squares into heart shapes.

Attach the Appliqués
5. Lay one sleeve of the cardigan flat and make sure it's positioned so that the lace hearts can be laid down where your actual elbows are. You may want to test this out by wearing the cardigan first and then placing some pins where you want the heart-shaped elbow patches to go.

6. After you know where you want to place the hearts, peel the paper backing off of one of the lace hearts and place it in position, lace side up. With the iron set to the silk setting, press down on the heart for 8 to 10 seconds. Check to see whether or not the heart has adhered and if not, carefully iron it a few more times until it does. Repeat this step with the other lace elbow patch.

7. When the elbow patches are done, make the lace collar. The process is exactly the same as the elbows except that you should use the collar template. If your collar is a different shape than the cardigan pictured, adjust the template accordingly.

PILLOWCASE TANK

What to do with a graphic pillowcase that's lost its mate? Make a low-sew tank!

DESIGNER:
Yuka Yoneda,
Clossette.com

STITCH FACTOR:

low sew

WHAT YOU'LL DO:
Simple sewing

figure 1

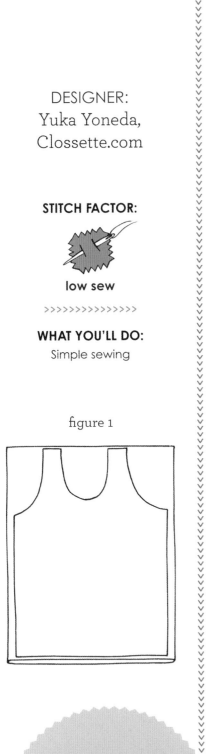

Skip the Stitching!

If you don't want to hem your edges (in step 4), leave them raw or apply a light coat of clear-drying fabric glue to the cut edges to seal them off.

You Will Need:

» A pillowcase
» A tank top you like, to use as a pattern
» Pencil
» Scissors
» Sewing machine or needle and thread (optional)
» Clear-drying fabric glue (optional)
» An iron and ironing surface

Cut the Outline

1. Turn the pillowcase inside out and lay it on a flat surface with the closed end at the top.

2. Find a tank top in your closet with a neckline that you like and lay it flat on top of the pillowcase. Line up the top of the tank top with the top (closed) end of the pillowcase. It's okay if the pillowcase is slightly wider than the tank top. Then use a pencil to lightly and carefully trace an outline of the neckline and armholes onto the pillowcase, leaving about a 1½ inches (3.8 cm) extra so that you will have room for a hem (figure 1). If you don't think your material will need a hem, just trace the shape exactly as it is on the tank top, using the top and side closed edges of the pillowcase.

3. Next, carefully cut along the lines you drew, making sure you don't cut the closed side edges or the sewn edges of the straps, which need to remain sewn together so that they become the shoulders of the tank.

Finish the Edges

4. Hem the edges of neckline and the armholes.

5. Finally, flip the new tank top so it's right side out, and press it. You can also adjust the length by cutting and hemming the bottom if you want to.

WOVEN CHEVRON COWL

Low-sew and cozy? Yes, please! Create this woven cowl with two tones of fleece and only a single seam at the back.

Only one seam!

STITCH FACTOR:

low sew

>>>>>>>>>>>>>

WHAT YOU'LL DO:
Cutting, weaving &
simple sewing

You Will Need:

- » ⅓ yard (30.5 cm) dark fleece
- » ⅓ yard (30.5 cm) light fleece
- » Craft knife
- » Craft mat
- » 1 sheet of transparency paper
- » Water-soluble fabric marker
- » Cutting template (page 124)
- » Sewing machine or needle and thread

figure 1

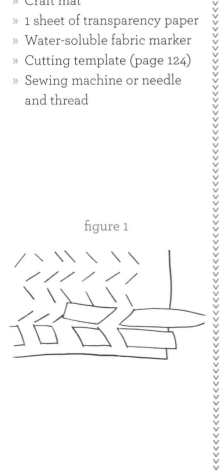

Cut the Panel & the Strips

1. Cut a panel from the dark fleece that measures 9 x 25 inches (22.9 x 63.5 cm).

2. Cut 6 strips from the light fleece that measure 1 x 25 inches (2.5 x 63.5 cm).

3. Lay the dark fleece panel out flat, and using the template, mark the slanted lines with the water-soluble fabric marker.

4. Continue marking the panel with the lines that are on the cutting template, spacing them about 1 inch (2.5 cm) apart.

5. Cut the slanted chevron lives open using the craft knife and the craft mat.

Weave the Fleece

6. Starting at one end, weave the light fleece stripes into the panel. Start each stripe on the same side of the panel to create the chevron pattern (figure 1).

7. Once all the strips have been woven into the panel, cut off the excess portion of the strips on both ends.

8. Baste the strips in place on both ends.

9. Bring the short ends of the panel together, and twist one end to create the mobius loop. Pin the ends together, and then stitch the ends with a ¼-inch (0.6 cm) seam allowance.

Wear

KNOTTED
FLEECE HAT

Because fleece's edges don't ravel, you can simply
cut and tie the edges together to create "seams."

DESIGNER:
Joan K. Morris

STITCH FACTOR:

no sew

>>>>>>>>>>>>>>

WHAT YOU'LL DO:
Cutting & tying

You Will Need:

» Ruler
» Scissors
» ½ yard (0.5 m) polka-dot fleece*
» ½ yard (0.5 m) cream fleece*
» Straight pins

*Note: *You can make two hats with this amount of fleece.*

figure 1

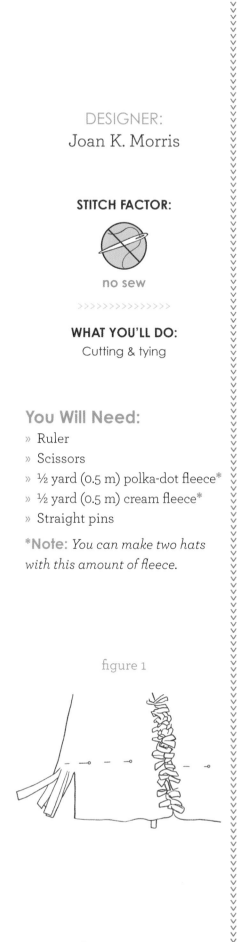

Prep the Fabric

1. Cut a piece of the polka-dot fleece and a piece of the cream fleece that measure 15 x 18 inches (38.1 x 45.7 cm).

2. Place the two pieces of fleece together.

Tip: *Fleece has no right side so it doesn't matter which sides are together.*

Cut & Tie the Slits

3. Along one of the 18-inch (45.7 cm) edges, measure in 2 inches (5.1 cm) and place straight pins to create a guide line. Cut ¼-inch-wide (0.6 cm) slits through both fleece layers, cutting up to the 2-inch (5.1 cm) mark and working all the way across the 18-inch (45.7 cm) edge.

4. Place the pieces in front of you with the cut edges of the strips facing each other. Start at the top and tie the strips from each side together. Knot the strips right over left, then left over right, and pull tight, but not too tight as the fleece might tear. Repeat this all the way down the edge. Trim the ends of the knots to ½ inch (1.3 cm).

5. Turn the piece over and repeat steps 3 and 4 on the other 18-inch (45.7 cm) edge.

Finish the Top Edge

6. Place the piece in front of you so one of the knotted seams is on top, with one side the polka dot and one side the cream. Measure up from the bottom edge 2 inches (5.1 cm), and place straight pins to create a guide line.

7. Cut ¼-inch strips (0.6 cm) from one edge to the other. In each corner, knot three strips together to create the tassels (figure 1).

8. Turn the piece inside out, and knot the remaining strips as you did in step 4. Trim the ends to ½ inch (1.3 cm).

9. Turn the hat right side out and fold up the bottom edge two times.

WOVEN
LEATHER CUFF

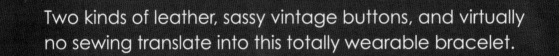

Two kinds of leather, sassy vintage buttons, and virtually no sewing translate into this totally wearable bracelet.

DESIGNER:
Cynthia Shaffer

STITCH FACTOR:

low sew

>>>>>>>>>>>>>

WHAT YOU'LL DO:
Cutting, weaving
& simple sewing

You Will Need:

» Masking tape
» Navy blue leather, 1¼ x
  6¼ inches (3.2 x 15.9 cm)
» Craft mat
» Template (page 124)
» Small ruler
» Craft knife
» White marker
» Small hole punch
» Leather cording in light blue,
  36 inches (91.4 cm)
» Large-eye hand-sewing needle
» Hand-sewing needle
» Peach perle cotton
» Vintage button, peach and
  gold colored

figure 1

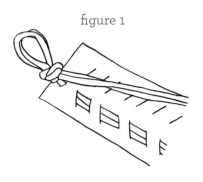

Skip the Stitching!
I love the stitched edge on this cuff. To get a similar effect–in much less time!–skip the overcast stitching in step 10, and cut a zigzag, scalloped, or other decorative design along the edges of the strip.

Cut the Leather Strip

1. Tape the leather strip to the craft mat. Tape the template on top of the leather strip.

2. Using the ruler and craft knife and the template as a guide, cut the little slits into the leather.

3. Mark the circle at the ends of the leather strip using the white marker.

4. Punch out the two holes on both ends of the leather strip. The third white mark on one end is where the button will be sewn.

Weave the Leather

5. Cut two strands of cording that measure 18 inches (45.7 cm), and knot the ends together. Using the large-eye needle and the leather cording, weave the cording in and out of the cut slits, starting from the wrong side.

6. When you reach the end of the strip, create a loop for the button by tying a knot in the leather cording (figure 1).

7. Continue weaving in and out of the leather strip on the opposite side.

8. When you reach the end, tie a knot in the leather cording on the wrong side and trim the excess off.

Finish the Edges

9. Hand-stitch an overcast stitch around the outer edge of the leather strip with the peach perle cotton.

10. Stitch a button to the one end where the white mark is.

33

Wear

SHIRT SKIRT

Find a boy's shirt, cut off the top, and sew a simple hem casing for the elastic band. Meet your new favorite upcycling project!

Used to be a shirt!

DESIGNER:

Cynthia Shaffer

STITCH FACTOR:

low sew

>>>>>>>>>>>>>>

WHAT YOU'LL DO:
Simple sewing &
adding buttons

You Will Need:

» Striped shirt with a straight
  bottom edge*
» Ruler
» Pencil
» Sewing machine
» Safety pin
» 22 inches (55.9 cm) of ¾-inch
  (1.9 cm) non-roll elastic
» Hand-sewing needle
» 4 brown buttons

*Note: *This project used a boy's
shirt, size 10/12.*

Prep the Shirt

1. Flatten the shirt, and using the ruler and a pencil, mark a line that runs from side seam to side seam, right where the sleeves are attached. Cut along this line through all layers.

Make the Pocket

2. Cut off one sleeve. From the detached sleeve portion, cut a rectangle that measures 5¼ x 6½ inches (13.3 x 16.5 cm) for the pocket. Use the finished sleeve hem as the side of the pocket.

3. Press all the cut edges under ¼ inch (0.6 cm).

4. Fold the top of the pocket down 1 inch (2.5 cm).

5. Stitch across the pocket hem ¾ inch (1.9 cm) from the top folded edge.

6. Stitch the pocket to the front of the skirt, 3 inches (7.6 cm) over from the button seam and 5 inches (12.7 cm) down from the top edge.

Create the Casing

7. Pin the front of the shirt closed at the top. If there is a button at the very top, remove the button.

8. Press the top edge under ¼ inch (0.6 cm) and then again another 1 inch (2.5 cm). Pin the waist down to the skirt. Place two pins at the center back, and then another two pins 2 inches (5.1 cm) away.

9. Stitch the top edge in place to create a casing for the elastic. Start stitching where the two pins are, back tack, then stop stitching when you reach the second set of pins and back tack.

10. Insert the safety pin into one end of the elastic, and then insert and feed the pin into the casing until you reach the end.

11. Pin and then stitch the elastic ends together.

12. Stitch closed the small opening at the center back.

13. Stitch the brown buttons to the front of the skirt and to the top of the pocket.

Tip: *Use an adult-sized shirt and the same basic steps to make a skirt for you.*

Wear

HEXAGON
ART TILE

I love a shortcut. With this pretty panel, you can have all the hexagon fun you want—no paper piecing necessary.

DESIGNER:
Jenny Bartoy

STITCH FACTOR:

no sew

>>>>>>>>>>>>>>

WHAT YOU'LL DO:
Gluing

figure 1

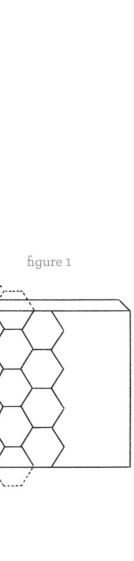

You Will Need:

» Iron and ironing surface
» 9 scraps of coordinating fabric, at least 3 inches (7.6 cm) square
» Spray fabric starch (optional)
» Template (page 120)
» Pencil or erasable pen
» Sharp scissors or rotary cutter and self-healing mat
» Wood art panel (available at most art supply stores), 8 inches (20.3 cm) square
» Digital camera (optional)
» Foam brush or small brayer
» Newspaper or drop cloth
» Mod Podge® Gloss-Lustre

Cut the Scraps

1. Press the fabric scraps.

Tip: *Starching the scraps helps you cut crisp shapes.*

2. Using the template, trace a hexagon shape on the back of each fabric scrap. If desired, include a cute or interesting aspect of the fabric design within the boundaries of the hexagon.

3. With sharp scissors or a rotary cutter and self-healing mat, carefully cut out each hexagon.

Arrange the Hexagons

4. Arrange the hexagons on the wood panel. Play with the placement of specific hexagons until the resulting patchwork is pleasing to your eye. If you cut the hexagons to exact measurements, the top and bottom edges of the right-hand column of hexagons should be flush with your panel edges, while the top and bottom hexagons on the left should fold straight down the middle to rest against the panel edges (figure 1). If necessary, trim each hexagon very carefully until the fit is right.

continued ——>

37

5. Take a digital photo or make a note of your final hexagon arrangement, then remove the hexagons from the wood panel.

6. Lay the bare wood panel on newspapers or a drop cloth. Using the foam brush or small brayer, cover it with a thin layer of Mod Podge®.

7. It's time to recreate your hexagon puzzle! Working quickly but neatly, transfer the hexagons to the panel. Begin toward the center of the panel with the right-hand column. Start with the top hexagon, flush with the edge, and work your way down. Next, place hexagons in the left column. Start with the middle hexagons and work your way to the top and bottom, carefully matching edges between the hexagons, one by one.

Tip: *If you find that the Mod Podge® has dried in certain spots, apply a bit more to the wood before placing the rest of the hexagons on the panel. Make sure that each hexagon lies smooth and flat, and that its edges are flush with its neighbors' edges. If you need to correct the placement of a hexagon, peel it off before the Mod Podge® has dried and reapply.*

8. Let the panel and fabric dry completely. If necessary, trim any errant threads.

Apply a Final Coat

9. With the foam brush or brayer, apply a generous coat of Mod Podge® over the whole panel, including the side edges. When going over the hexagons, work gently so as not to fray the fabric edges.

10. Once again, let the panel and fabric dry, then repeat step 9 to completely seal the panel. Once the panel is dry, your artwork is done!

Never Been Stitched

ROUND ROBIN RUG

This sweet little low-sew rug will add a pop of color in your bedroom, your favorite nook, or wherever it's needed.

DESIGNER: Jessica Fediw

You Will Need:

- Canvas or decorator fabric for the top (see step 1 below)
- Coordinating canvas or decorator fabric for the bottom (see step 1 below)
- Iron and ironing surface
- Yardstick or measuring tape
- Chalk
- Sharp scissors
- Pompom trim (see step 6 below)
- Straight pins
- Sewing machine with coordinating thread
- Fabric and upholstery protector spray (optional)

STITCH FACTOR:

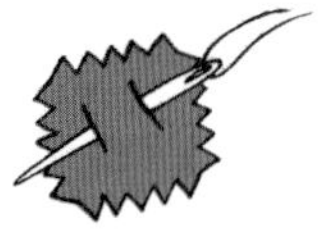

low sew

>>>>>>>>>>>>>>>

WHAT YOU'LL DO:

Simple sewing

Cut the Rug

1. Determine the desired size of your rug first. It can only be as wide as the fabric. Make sure that you buy the yardage that equals the width of the fabric you have chosen; for example, if you're making a rug 45 inches (114.3 cm) wide, you will need 1¼ yards, which equals 45 inches (114.3 cm). The bottom fabric needs to be the same yardage and at least the same width.

Tip: *Use an outdoor decorator fabric for an outdoor rug or for a more durable inside rug.*

2. Fold the rug top fabric in half, and then fold it in half again widthwise. Two sides will be fabric folds, and two will be raw edges.

3. Divide the desired width by two (for example, 34 inches [86.4 cm] ÷ 2 = 17 inches [43.2 cm]). Take a yardstick or measuring tape and place one end on the corner where the two folded sides meet. Make a mark with the chalk on the half measurement (e.g., 17 inches [43.2 cm]). Keeping the end of the ruler in the same place, move the other end to create more marks that equal the same length from one side to the other (figure 1).

figure 1

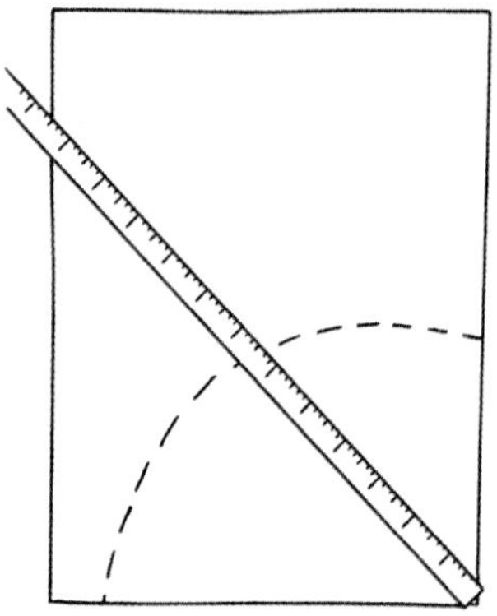

4. Now connect the marks you made with the chalk to make a quarter circle. Cut along that line. Open up the full circle.

5. Repeat steps 2 to 4 on the bottom fabric.

Add the Trim

6. To determine the amount of pompom trim you need, calculate the circumference of your rug by multiplying the diameter (the desired width, or, in the example above, mulitply 45 inches [114.3 cm]) by 3.14, or pi; in this case 141^5/$_{16}$ inches (358.9 cm). Then add a few extra inches (or centimeters) to that number just to be on the safe side. Place the top fabric on the floor, right side up, and pin the pompom trim along the edges. Make sure the pompoms face the inside of the fabric.

7. Sew the trim in place (figure 2).

Add the Backing

8. Place the bottom fabric on the floor right side up. Then put the top fabric on it, wrong side up, matching the edges. Pin together.

9. Sew around the fabric edges, leaving about a 10-inch (25.4 cm) opening. Sew a little closer to the fabric edge from where you sewed the trim on. Just make sure not to sew through the pompoms.

10. Pull the fabric through the opening to turn it right side out. Then push on the seams from the inside using your hand.

11. Tuck in the edges at the opening so it's even with the rest of the rug edge and pin.

12. Sew around the top edge to close the opening and secure the fabrics.

Tip: *If you're not using outdoor fabric, you can spray your rug with a fabric and upholstery protector spray.*

figure 2

QUEEN ANNE'S
LACE PANELS

Turn your favorite flower into abstract wall art. These flowers
are fused on linen and stretched over canvas art panels.

DESIGNER:

Amanda Carestio

STITCH FACTOR:

no sew

>>>>>>>>>>>>>

WHAT YOU'LL DO:
Fused appliqué

You Will Need:

» Pencil
» Templates (page 121)
» Paper-backed fusible web,
   ½ yard (45.7 cm)
» Iron and ironing surface
» ½ yard (45.7 cm) of fabric
   for stems and flowers
» Sharp scissors
» Circle shape, ¾ inch (1.9 cm)
   in diameter, to trace for the
   flower-bud template
» Piece of fabric for the flower
   buds, 5 x 15 inches (12.7 x 38.1 cm)
» 2 canvas panels, 12 x 16 inches
   (30.5 x 40.6 cm) each
» 1 yard (.9 m) of fabric for the
   background
» Ruler or tape measure
» Rotary cutter and self-healing
   mat (optional)
» Staple gun and staples

Create the Appliqués

1. Trace the flower template onto the fusible web's paper backing two times. Following the manufacturer's instructions, fuse it to the wrong side of the stem and flower fabric, and cut out the shapes.

2. Trace the ¾-inch (1.9 cm) circle shape 30 times onto fusible web's paper backing. Fuse the webbing to the wrong side of the bud fabric. Cut out the shapes, remove the paper backing, and cut out a center circle from each bud shape. Don't worry too much about creating perfect circles in this step.

3. Fuse a 15 x 6-inch (38.1 x 15.2 cm) section of webbing to the wrong side of the remaining stem and flower fabric, and set aside; these will become the stems.

Cut the Backgrounds

4. Measure the canvas panels. Add 6 inches (15.2 cm) to each dimension, and use these measurements to cut the background fabric. For this project, the panels are 12 x 16 inches (30.5 x 40.6 cm), so you'll cut two background rectangles that measure 18 x 22 inches (47.6 x 55.9 cm).

Fuse the Flowers

5. Lay the background fabric loosely over the canvas panels and position the flower appliqué shapes as desired.

6. Measure the distances from the flowers to the bottom edge of the background fabric, and cut the stems to these lengths using the fabric you set aside in step 3. Simple strips will do, or to create slightly curved stems, try using a rotary cutter.

7. Following the manufacturer's instructions, fuse the layers in place, starting with the stems, then the flowers, and finally adding the little bud circles.

Stretch and Staple the Panels

8. Center the fused panels on the canvas panels, wrap the excess fabric to the back, and staple in place. Start with the two long edges and then move to the shorter edges, folding over the corners as you work.

PRETTY PLACEMAT PILLOWS

Give the lowly placemat new life on the couch. With no edges to finish, you can have these pillows done before company comes.

Hey, look: no stitching!

DESIGNER:
Rebeka Lambert

STITCH FACTOR:

no sew

>>>>>>>>>>>>>

WHAT YOU'LL DO:
Fusing

You Will Need:

» Seam ripper
» Double-sided placemat (constructed of two pieces of fabric sewn together)
» Polyester fiberfill
» Fusible web tape
» Iron and ironing surface

Open the Placemat

1. Using the seam ripper, gently undo the seam along one side of the placemat, making an opening of approximately 5 to 6 inches (12.7 to 15.2 cm). The best location for this is at the middle of one of the long sides.

Fill the Pillow

2. Stuff polyester fiberfill through the opening to fill the placemat to your desired fullness.

3. Cut a piece of fusible web tape slightly longer than your opening. Position the webbing along the opening, then seal using your iron and following the manufacturer's instructions.

45

STYLISH
STORAGE BOXES

Dress up your closet or keep your craft corner in order. These storage boxes make the most of burlap, felt, and thrifted stitched panels.

DESIGNER:
Suzie Millions

STITCH FACTOR:

no sew

>>>>>>>>>>>>>>

WHAT YOU'LL DO:
Cutting, gluing & knotting

You Will Need:

» Clear packing tape
» Cardboard box
» Cutting mat
» Straightedge
» Craft knife
» Ruler or measuring tape
» Bone folder (use the back
  of a scissors blade if you
  don't have one)
» Scissors
» Burlap
» Stack of newspaper
  (at least six layers)
» Spray adhesive
» Stiff board
» Needlework, removed
  from the frame
» Painter's tape
» Bright felt from the roll
» Piece of burlap, 10 x 4 inches
  (25.4 x 10.2 cm)
» 15 inches (38.1 cm) of round
  cord, for the pull handle
» Hot glue gun and glue sticks

Cover the Box

1. Add some clear packing tape to the bottom of the box to make it extra sturdy.

2. Put the box upside down on the cutting mat with the flaps splayed out and trim them with the straight-edge and craft knife to 1¼ inches (3.2 cm). Make a crease on each flap about ⅛ inch (3 mm) from the fold using the straightedge and bone folder. With your thumb on the inside of the box, wrap your fingers over the bottom edge of each flap and pull up, creating a small ridge where the flap meets the box top, to help the flaps lay flat.

3. Measure all the way around the outside of the box and cut a piece of burlap ½ inch (1.3 cm) taller than the side panels, and long enough to wrap around with 1 inch (2.5 cm) of overlap. Measure the bottom of the box and cut a piece of burlap to size. Don't worry about edges fraying or pattern-perfect cutting—burlap is pretty forgiving.

4. Lay down several layers of newspaper in the area where you're going to use the spray adhesive. Put the burlap panels somewhere safe from overspray, but nearby and at the ready; they need to be added on the box when the spray is very tacky. Tuck the flaps into the box and put it upside down on the newspapers. Spray each side and the bottom lightly with spray adhesive.

5. Starting at the center of the back panel, with the top of the burlap just below the top of the box and the overage at the bottom, wrap the burlap around the box, pulling it snug and smoothing as you go. You should end up where you started with about 1 inch (2.5 cm) of overlap. Smooth the excess over the bottom of the box. Pull a few threads off of the edge of the vertical seam in the center of the back panel to make some fringe. If your seam flaps at all, it might be too long. Trim and fringe it again.

6. Smooth the bottom panel of burlap onto the box, first lightly until you're sure it's positioned right, and

continued ⟶

then firmly after you're sure it's lined up. Pull a couple of threads off the edges on all sides to make a small fringe. If the fringe sticks out more than ⅛ inch (3 mm) or so from the bottom of the box, trim it.

Create the Needlework Panel

7. Cut a piece of stiff board an inch (2.5 cm) shorter and narrower than the front panel of the box. Position the needlework over the stiff board to figure out how you want to crop it. On the back of the needlework, put a long piece of painter's tape on just one side of the board to hold it in place. Carefully put it needlework-side-down on clean newspaper. Using the tape as a hinge, gently flip the board over, spray it heavily, pause for a few seconds to let it get more tacky than wet, then fold it back down onto the needlework. Press firmly over the back of the board, and then flip it over and smooth out any wrinkles. Trim the needlework to be the same size as the board using the cutting mat, craft knife, and straightedge. Using a firm hand and a brand new blade will help keep the cuts as crisp and clean as possible. Spray the board with adhesive and position the needlework on the front of the box, about ½ inch (1.3 cm) from all the edges.

Line the Box

8. Cut seven pieces of felt (figure 1):

• One long panel that will go from front to back, covering the inside bottom panel
Length: (box height x 2) + box depth + (flap height x 2) + (½ inch [1.3 cm] underlap x 2) + 1 inch (2.5 cm) leeway
Width: width of the inside of the box + ¼ inch (6 mm)

• Two medium panels for the sides
Length: box height + flap height + 1½ inches (3.8 cm)
Width: depth of the box

• Four small panels for the epaulets on the outside corners: 2 x 6 inches (5.1 x 15.2 cm)

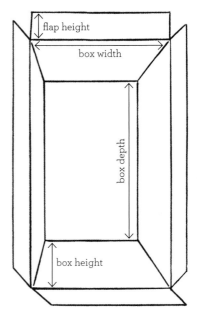

figure 1

Never Been Stitched

9. Turn the flaps inside the box, so the backs are facing up, and spray the back of the flaps. Turn them toward the outside and spray the inside of the box and the flap fronts. If you rotate the box as you spray so that you're always spraying the panel facing you, you can avoid getting spray on the outside of the box where you don't want it.

10. Put the felt side panels in first. Start with the front of the flap, leaving ½ inch (1.3 cm) on the outside edge to tuck under later, and smooth it over the ridge on top of the flap and down the inside of the box. Reposition and tug until it reaches the corner on both sides and spills onto the bottom by about ¼ inch (6 mm). Smooth it down and press it into all the corners. Smooth over the edge and under the flap. Repeat for the other side.

11. Next, affix the long front-to-back panel. Start on the front flap, leaving ½ inch (1.3 cm) on the edge to tuck under later. Smooth it over the ridge on top of the flap, down the inside of the front panel, pushing it deeply into the crease where the front panel meets the bottom. Smooth it over the bottom, deeply into the crease between the bottom and the back panel, up the back panel, and over the back flap. Reposition it if you need to. It should overlap the edges of the side panels slightly so no cardboard is showing. Smooth the excess under the flaps.

Add the Handles

12. To attach the pull handle on the front, measure the width of the front panel, and make a mark 1½ inches (3.8 cm) to the right of the center and ¾ inch (1.9 cm) from the top edge (figure 8). Push the craft knife deeply through it, from the front of the box through the felt lining. Make an X-shaped cut with the craft knife. Push the back of the craft knife all the way through the X to make a circular hole, keeping your hand inside the box to support the felt while you push. Repeat this on the left side. Tie a knot at one end of the pull-handle cord, large

continued ⟶

Decorate

enough to keep it secure on the inside of the box. Wrap a small piece of painter's tape around the other end of the cord. Push the cord through the box from the inside to the outside, then through the other hole from the outside to the inside. Pull the knot tight to the inside wall and arrange the cord until there is a loop on the front of the box about 2½ inches (6.4 cm) deep. Mark or hold the cord to indicate where the second knot should be. Pull extra cord into the box so you can make the second knot. Tug it tightly, then pull the loop on the front back into place, with the second knot tight against the inside wall, too. Trim the ends of the knots closely.

Tip: *To keep the ends of the knot neat and to prevent them from pulling through, put a blob of hot glue on the ends, then press the ends down against the knot.*

13. Glue the flaps down. One at a time, put a heavy bead of hot glue on the back of the flap, zigzagging up and down; keep the glue at least ½ inch (1.3 cm) from the edge so no glue oozes out. Wait until the glue sets just a little, then press the flap down, holding with both hands. Press hard so that the glue makes it through the burlap and onto the box for a better bind.

14. To make the epaulets, fold one of the small pieces of felt in half crosswise, matching the shorter ends. Fringe the end opposite the fold by making cuts 1¼ inches (3.2 cm) deep and about ³⁄₁₆ inch (5 mm) wide. Pull three long threads of burlap from the 10 x 4-inch (25.4 x 10.2 cm) piece. Wrap them around the folded felt, midway, where the fringe begins. Cinch the felt by knotting the threads tightly, then knot them again. Tug the corners of the unfringed end to widen the epaulet, then trim the ends of the burlap strings even with the fringe. Make all four epaulets, pick the two best, and put those on the front of the box. Put a bead of hot glue on the top back of the epaulet, and another blob midway down on the back of the threads, and put it on the top corner of the box, straddling the gap between the flaps. Align the top first, press it down, then press and hold the center for a few seconds.

Never Been Stitched

MERRY NO-SEW ORNAMENT

No-sew your way to a merry holiday! Pin folded fabric squares onto a foam form to create this lovely snow-capped tree ornament.

You Will Need:

» 1 rectangle of green fabric, 9½ x 2½ inches (24.1 x 6.4 cm), to cover the base of the tree
» 1 polystyrene cone, 8½ inches (21.6 cm) high and 2¾ inches (7 cm) in diameter
» Head pins
» Sharp scissors
» Ribbon or some other embellishment to cover the treetop
» Scraps of assorted green fabrics cut into three sizes: 3 inches (7.6 cm) square, 2½ inches (6.4 cm) square, and 2 inches (5.1 cm) square*
» Scraps of assorted white and cream fabrics cut into two sizes: 2 inches (5.1 cm) square and 1½ inches (3.8 cm) square

*Notes: *You will need approximately 10 fabric squares per row for the first six rows. For the next two rows you'll need 9 squares, then 8, then 6, and so on (figure 1). Cut a mix of green and white 2-inch (5.1 cm) squares but only whites and creams for the 1½-inch (3.8 cm) squares. Using a mix of greens and whites will achieve a gradual transition from green to white to simulate a snowy treetop.*

Cover the Base

1. Wrap the 9½ x 2½-inch (24.1 x 6.4 cm) green fabric rectangle around the bottom of the tree and pin it on each side. Gather the fabric at the bottom and pin to the base of the cone, making sure the fabric is as flat as possible. Trim any excess fabric to reduce the bulk if necessary to ensure the tree stands flush with the surface and doesn't wobble.

Fold the Squares

2. To form the fabric squares, fold a square of green fabric in half, then fold it in half again to make a square. No need to iron; just run your fingers across the crease.

DESIGNER:
Teresa Mairal Barreu

STITCH FACTOR:

no sew

>>>>>>>>>>>>>>

WHAT YOU'LL DO:
Folding & pinning

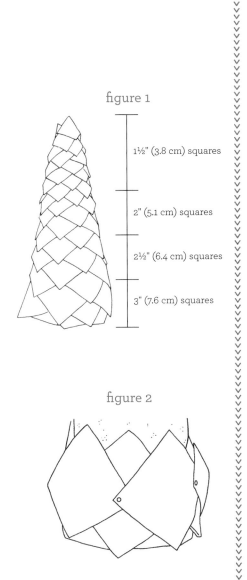

figure 1

1½" (3.8 cm) squares

2" (5.1 cm) squares

2½" (6.4 cm) squares

3" (7.6 cm) squares

figure 2

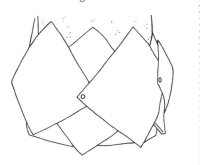

Pin the Rows

3. To make the first row, pin two rows of the squares formed in step 2 around the cone. First, place the squares on point, slightly overlapping the corners, and pin. You will need to use five squares to do this (figure 1).

4. Once you've covered the full circumference of the cone, you need to use another five squares and place the squares on point, making sure the point falls in between the space left by two squares in the previous circle (figure 2). This completes one row.

5. Repeat steps 2 through 4 to complete a second row.

6. After you complete a second row in the same way, start using 2½-inch (6.4 cm) squares and complete two more rows.

7. Use the 2-inch (5.1 cm) squares next and start adding cream, white, and beige squares every now and then to simulate snow.

8. As you start using 1½-inch (3.8 cm) squares, add only creams for the snow.

9. For the last couple of rows, you'll need fewer squares to go around the circle.

10. To cover the treetop, use a ribbon and a bow, or see the suggested variations below.

Make It Your Own

Turn your tree into a wedding ornament by changing the fabric colors; simply use silver or any other color that matches the wedding color scheme. Or instead of using cotton fabric squares, use ribbon; you only need to fold the ribbon in half once because ribbon is hemmed on each side. You can also use the same idea and technique to cover other foam shapes. Visit LarkCrafts.com to download instructions for this Christmas Ball Ornament.

53

NO-MESS MESSAGE CENTER

This little hoop makes the perfect home for your daily reminders, notes, and quick messages.

DESIGNER:
Joan K. Morris

STITCH FACTOR:

no sew

>>>>>>>>>>>>>>

WHAT YOU'LL DO:
Gluing

You Will Need:

» Piece of background fabric, 16 inches (40.6 cm) square (you could use a scrap of fabric you have on hand or a quilting square)
» Iron and ironing surface
» Wooden embroidery hoop, 12 inches (30.5 cm) in diameter
» Scissors
» Fabric glue
» Piece of pocket fabric, 16 inches (40.6 cm) square
» 5 yards (4.6 m) of ribbon, ¼ inch (6 mm) wide
» Ruler
» Straight pins

Prep the Background

1. Press the background fabric with the iron. Center the inside ring of the embroidery hoop on the wrong side of the pressed background fabric. Turn the fabric and hoop over and, from the front, slide the outside of the embroidery hoop over the fabric and the inside hoop. Tighten the outside hoop in place.

2. Pull the fabric tight from the wrong side and then cut the fabric around the edge ½ inch (1.3 cm) from the hoop.

3. Squeeze a bead of glue, working a few inches at a time, around the inside of the hoop, fold the fabric to the inside, and press it in place. Let the glue dry. Remove the outside ring.

Add the Ribbons

4. Cut 10 pieces of the ribbon, each 16 inches (40.6 cm) long. Place five pieces of ribbon on the right side of the hoop with one piece centered and the others 2 inches (5.1 cm) apart and parallel to the center. Pin them in place on one side.

continued ⟶

5. Place the other five ribbon pieces across and perpendicular to the first five, again spaced 2 inches (5.1 cm) apart. At this point, weave the ribbons over and under so that notes can be placed between the ribbons (figure 1).

6. Remove the pins and carefully slide the outside ring in place over the ribbon. Tighten the ring slightly, adjust the ribbons, and the tighten the outside ring again. Place dabs of glue on the inside of the ring, place the end of the ribbon in the glue, and press them with your finger. Repeat this on all ribbon ends and let the glue dry.

Make the Pocket

7. Fold the pocket fabric in half with wrong sides together, making a 16 x 8-inch (40.6 x 20.3 cm) piece. Press with the iron.

8. Remove the outside ring. On the right side, position the pocket so that the distance from the folded pocket edge to the bottom edge of the ring is 5 to 5½ inches (12.7 to 14 cm).

9. Turn the whole thing over and mark 2 inches (5.1 cm) out from the hoop in a circle on the pocket fabric (figure 2).

10. Cut along the line you drew in step 9.

11. Put the pocket in position, place the outer hoop over everything, and tighten it in place.

12. Run a line of glue on the inside edge of the hoop where the pocket will fold over. Fold the pocket ends to the inside over the glue and press in place with your fingers (figure 3). Let the glue dry, hang your message center, and insert a pad of paper and pens.

figure 1

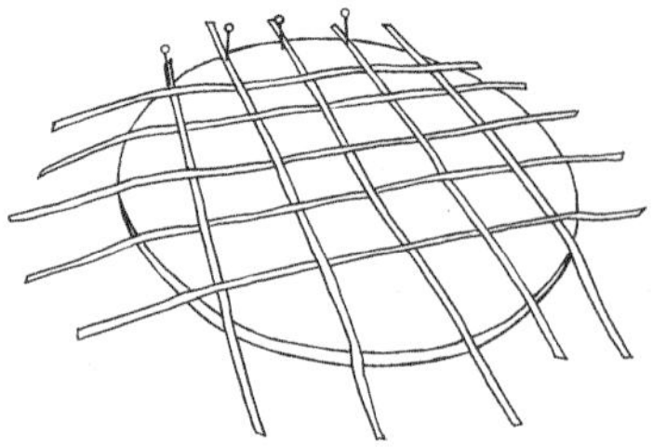

figure 2

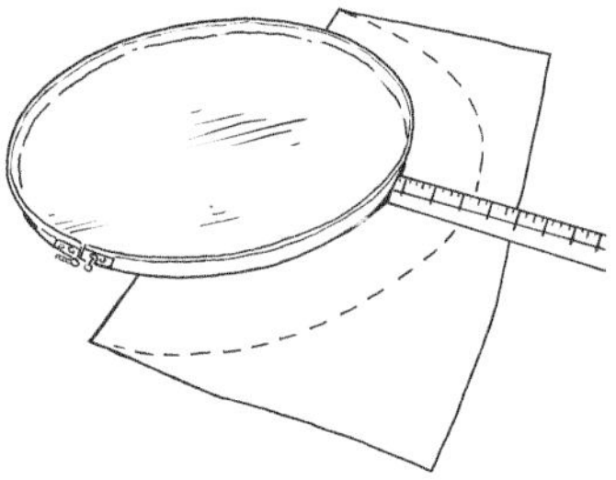

figure 3

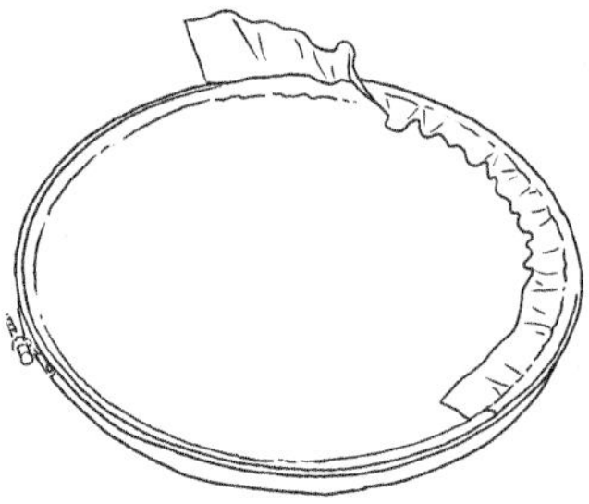

ROMAN SHADE

Even better with a large-scale print fabric, this easy shade is polished and pretty. Just adjust the measurements to fit your window.

You Will Need:

» 2 yards (1.8 m) of fabric for the front of the shade (not stretchy or too heavy)*
» 2 yards (1.8 m) of lining fabric
» Measuring tape
» Straight pins
» Sharp scissors
» Iron and ironing board
» Super-weight fusible web tape, ⅝ inch (1.6 cm) wide
» Pen or knitting needle
» 7 yards (6.4 m) of grosgrain ribbon to coordinate with the shade's front fabric, 1½ inches (3.8 cm) wide
» Fray retardant
» Curtain rod or dowel

*Note: *These instructions are for a 32 x 60-inch (81.3 x 152.4 cm) shade. It's easy to adjust for a different size window: just measure your window and add or subtract the difference from the measurements here.*

Make the Panel

1. If you plan on washing your shade at some point, prewash the fabric before you cut it out.

2. Cut the fabric for the front to measure 33 x 64 inches (83.8 x 162.6 cm). If there is a large pattern to the fabric, make sure you center the pattern before you cut.

3. Lay the cut front fabric and the curtain lining fabric right sides together, lining up one of the edges of the front with the selvage edge of the curtain lining. Pin the fabrics together. Cut the lining to exactly the same size as the front fabric.

4. Place one 33-inch (83.8 cm) end of the pinned fabric on the ironing board. Measure out an 8-inch (20.3 cm) opening in the center of this short end. Place the fusible web tape in between the front fabric and the lining (figure 1), starting at one end of the 8-inch (20.3 cm) opening. Press it in place following the manufacturer's instructions, pressing 10 to 12 inches (25.4 to 30.5 cm)

DESIGNER:
Joan K. Morris

STITCH FACTOR:

no sew

>>>>>>>>>>>>>>

WHAT YOU'LL DO:
Fusing

figure 1

at a time and not cutting the fusible web tape until you reach the corners. Once you reach a corner, turn the piece over and press from the other side.

5. Go all the way around the fabric piece until you reach the other end of the 8-inch (20.3 cm) opening.

6. Turn the piece right side out through the 8-inch (20.3 cm) opening. Push out all of the corners with a closed pen or knitting needle. Press the whole piece flat, making sure the edges are even.

7. Close the 8-inch (20.3 cm) opening hole by inserting another piece of fusible web tape and pressing according to the manufacturer's instructions.

Attach the Ribbon

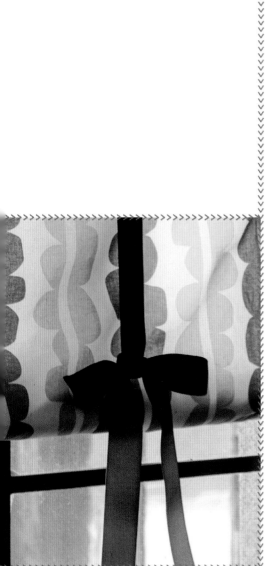

8. Cut the ribbon in half so you have two 3½-yard (3.2 m) pieces. Place a straight pin in the lengthwise center of each ribbon piece, dividing the ribbon into two 1¾-yard (1.6 m) halves. On the top edge of the shade measure in 8 inches (20.3 cm) from each side edge and then 3 inches (7.6 cm) down from the top edge. Place the pinned center of the ribbon on that spot, with half of the ribbon falling to the front of the fabric and the other half to the lining.

9. Cut two pieces of the fusible web tape 1½ inches (3.8 cm) long (the width of the ribbon). Place one piece of the fusible web tape under the pinned center of one ribbon and press both sides. Repeat with the other piece of webbing and the remaining ribbon.

Add the Curtain Rod

10. Measure down from the top edge of the shade 3 inches (7.6 cm) and fold it to the back. Cut another piece of fusible web tape that measures the width of the shade, and use it to press this edge in place, creating the pocket for the curtain rod.

11. Insert the curtain rod and hang the shade. You can roll the bottom edge up and tie the ribbon or fold it up and tie the ribbon. It's up to you.

59

MAP BUNTING

Don't stitch this!

Repurpose old maps into a fun and cheery bunting. Use star stickers to map out a vacation or to highlight your favorite locations.

DESIGNER:
Ginger Nolker

STITCH FACTOR:

no sew

>>>>>>>>>>>>>>

WHAT YOU'LL DO:
Gluing

You Will Need:

» Maps
» Scissors
» Ruler or tape measure
» Cellophane tape
» Fishing line
» Glue stick
» Foil star stickers (optional)
» Hooks or thumbtacks for hanging
» Clothespins or other clips for hanging artwork (optional)

Cut the Shapes

1. Unfold your map. Lay it out on the floor lengthwise. Use the long fold lines as guides to cut long strips from the map, approximately 8 inches (20.3 cm) wide.

2. Fold each strip in half lengthwise, with the side of the strip you wish to see facing out.

3. Cut triangles out of the strips, leaving a 3- to 4-inch (7.6 to 10.2 cm) base.

Join the Bunting

4. Once you have cut out all of the triangles, tape the strips together end to end to form the bunting. Trim to desired length.

5. Cut a length of fishing line that is as long as your bunting plus a 10-inch (25.4 cm) allowance on each end for hanging.

6. Unfold the bunting, inserting the fishing line along the fold. You can tape it in place if you like, but it isn't necessary.

7. Fold the bunting down again, and use the glue stick to glue the bunting together. You'll be gluing the triangles; make sure the fishing line stays inside the bunting along the top fold.

8. Add star stickers to mark places you have visited or other significant sites on the map, if desired.

9. Hang your bunting using the extra allowance of fishing line on each end. You can put hooks or tacks in the walls, and tie the fishing line around them. If you are going to hang artwork, be sure to stretch the fishing line tightly.

Make It Your Own

Cut different shapes to create different kinds of buntings! Simple animal shapes, stars, or circles could become fun mobiles.

61

PAPER-CUT PLACEMATS

With a hot two-tone color palette and a subtle floral pattern, these pretty placemats are feminine, modern, and useful.

DESIGNER:

Joan K. Morris

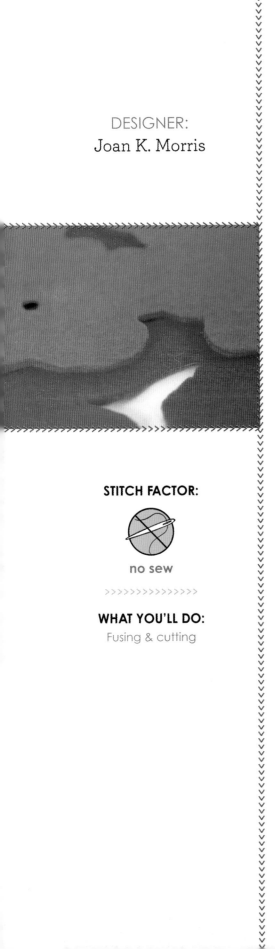

STITCH FACTOR:

no sew

>>>>>>>>>>>>>>

WHAT YOU'LL DO:
Fusing & cutting

You Will Need:

» Very sharp fabric scissors
» ½ yard (0.5 m) of pink felt
» ½ yard (0.5 m) of orange felt
» Iron-on adhesive (make sure the roll is at least 13 inches [33 cm] wide)
» Iron and ironing board
» Template (page 122)
» Paper and pencil for making the flower patterns
» Dressmaker pencil (white chalk)

Prep the Layers

1. Cut two pieces of pink felt to 13 x 17 inches (33 x 43.2 cm). Cut two pieces of orange felt to the same dimensions.

2. Cut two pieces of the iron-on adhesive to 12 x 16 inches (30.5 x 40.6 cm).

3. Following the manufacture's instructions, sandwich the iron-on adhesive between the pink and orange felt layers and fuse the layers together.

4. Cut the fused felt to the size of the iron-on adhesive.

Cut the Flower Shapes

5. Using the template, transfer the design with the dressmaker's pencil, working in small sections at a time to avoid rubbing the marks off while you work.

6. Cut around the template pattern, rubbing off the chalk lines as you complete each section.

Tip: *To cut the inside pieces, fold the felt, cut into the fold, open it up, and cut around the chalk line.*

Sweet, simple, and no sewing!

FABRIC-WRAPPED WREATH

Perfect for precuts or leftover strips from other projects, this wreath is also pretty in solids or in themed colors for holidays.

DESIGNER:
Cynthia Shaffer

STITCH FACTOR:

no sew

>>>>>>>>>>>>>>>

WHAT YOU'LL DO:
Wrapping
& pinning

You Will Need:

» Polyester quilt batting,
7 x 32 inches (17.8 x 81.3 cm)
» 10-inch (25.4 cm) foam wreath
» Quilter's T pins, 1¼ inch
(3.2 cm)
» 19 fabric strips, 2 x 20 inches
(5.1 x 50.8 cm) in a rainbow
of colors*
» ¾-inch (1.9 cm) sequin pins
» One fabric scrap strip, ¾ x 20
inches (1.9 x 50.8 cm)
» Hot glue
» Rubber elephant (or other
small toy)

*Note: *To create the rainbow
gradation, you'll need three or
four fabrics in each color. For
example, for red, you'll need four
small prints: one strip in red, one
in red and pink, one in pink, and
one in light pink. Continue in this
manner for the other colors—orange, yellow, green, blue, and
purple—as you work your way
around the wreath.*

Prep the Wreath

1. Wrap the panel of batting around the wreath, overlapping at the inside. Secure with the T pins.

Wrap the Strips

2. Start wrapping the red fabric strips around the
wreath, starting at the back, securing the strip with a
sequin pin.

3. Continue wrapping the red strip, overlapping the
first wrap by about ½ inch (1.3 cm).

4. When the red strip comes to the end at the back
of the wreath, pick up the next color, secure it with a
sequin pin, and then continue to wrap the strip around
the wreath.

Tip: *If you're working with shorter strips, simply start
and stop them on the back of the wreath, using pins to
secure the ends.*

5. Continue adding strips until you get to the last one.
In the sample, the last strip is dark purple. Cut this
strip in half lengthwise. Wrap the narrow purple strip
around the wreath and secure the end in the back with
a sequin pin.

6. Gently pull the first strip of red fabric out and over
the last purple strip. This will make all the strips look
uniform in width and will hide the starting and stop-
ping points!

7. From a scrap, tear a strip of fabric that measures
¾ x 20 inches (1.9 x 50.8 cm). Tie the strip around the
wreath to form the hanger.

Tip: *Cut the strip for step 7 from the same fabric that is
at the top of the wreath so that the hanger loop blends in
with the wreath.*

8. Hot glue the rubber elephant (or other small toy) to
the inside of the wreath at the bottom.

TOTE-N-THROW PILLOW

Got more totes than you can carry? Clever cutting and a single sewn seam transform a kitschy bag into a comfy pillow.

DESIGNER:
Yuka Yoneda,
Clossette.com

STITCH FACTOR:

low sew

>>>>>>>>>>>>>

WHAT YOU'LL DO:
Simple sewing

figure 1

figure 2

Skip the Stitching!
Create and finish the seam for the top of the pillow (step 4 and 7) with fusible web tape instead.

You Will Need:

» A tote bag with a design or logo you like
» Ruler
» Pencil
» Scissors
» Needle and thread
» Polyester fiberfill stuffing (or shred your own recycled fabric as filling)

Prep the Tote

1. Lay the tote bag flat so that the design or logo is facing up. Try to imagine the bag as a pillow and eyeball where you would want the top of it to be. Use a ruler and pencil to draw a very faint line across that area. Then draw a second line ½ inch (1.3 cm) above the first line (figure 1).

2. Step back from the newly marked-up tote bag and make sure you like the proportions. Once you like what you see, cut along the top line that you drew (the lower line will be where you stitch later).

3. Next, turn the bag inside out and lay it flat. Grab the ruler again and measure ½ inch (1.3 cm) down from the cut edge and draw a line across the tote. (Basically, you're duplicating your lower line from step 1 onto the inner surface of the tote so you have a guideline for your stitches.)

4. Using the needle and thread, stitch across the new line you just drew, leaving about 3 inches (7.6 cm) at the end (or enough to flip the bag right side out again and insert your stuffing later) (figure 2). Make a knot.

5. Flip the tote right side out.

Stuff the Pillow

6. Insert the stuffing until the fluffiness of the pillow is just right.

7. Tuck in the raw edges of the 3-inch (7.6 cm) opening you left for stuffing and stitch it shut.

Decorate

HOOPED
HANGING LAMP

Created from embroidery hoops and altered fabric, this
homemade shade makes a subtle yet stylish statement.

DESIGNER:

Joan K. Morris

STITCH FACTOR:

no sew

>>>>>>>>>>>>>>

WHAT YOU'LL DO:
Altering fabric
& fusing

You Will Need:

» ½ yard (0.5 m) fabric*
» Pins
» Bleach pen with a small point
» Iron and ironing board
» Two 7-inch (17.8 cm) wood embroidery hoops
» Super-weight fusible web tape, ⅝ inch (1.6 cm) wide
» Jute string
» Hot glue gun and glue
» Hanging lantern kit

*Note: *Natural fabrics and fibers seem to respond best to bleach.*

Prep the Fabric

1. Test your fabric to see how it will work with the bleach. The bleach may take a while to affect the fabric. Test both thin lines and thick lines.

2. Cut out a piece of fabric that measures 14 x 24 inches (35.6 x 61 cm).

3. Measure and use pins to mark a line 3 inches (7.6 cm) up from the bottom on a long edge. This is where you will start the design.

Create Your Design

4. Lay the fabric on a flat surface with plastic underneath; a garbage bag will work just fine. Draw your design with the bleach pen, working from the pinned line in step 3 up to 2 inches (5.1 cm) from the top all the way across the fabric, leaving an inch (2.5 cm) on each side. Let dry.

continued ⟶

69

Decorate

Hoop the Fabric

5. On one short end, fold under one edge and iron to create a hem.

6. Wrap the piece around the inside hoop of the embroidery hoop so that one short end slightly overlaps the other; this will help you figure out where to adhere the sides together. Use the fusible web tape to fuse the sides together, making a tube of fabric.

7. Cut 3 pieces of the jute string to 1 yard (0.9 m) each. Tie one end of the string to the outer ring of one of the embroidery hoops. Tie on the other two lengths of string so that the three are an equal distant apart and with the knots to the top.

8. Place the top of the fabric over the inside ring of the embroidery hoop, leaving 1 inch (2.5 cm) overlapping. Place the outer ring (from step 7) over the inner ring. Tighten the outer ring and adjust the fabric.

9. Place the bottom edge of the fabric on the inner ring of the other hoop. Secure the outer ring around it, tighten slightly, and adjust the fabric.

Create a Hanging Loop

10. Measure 8 inches (20.3 cm) up the jute strings from the ring and tie a knot connecting all three strings. From the knot, braid the jute for 12 inches (30.5 cm), and tie a knot. Fold the end over, creating a 1½-inch (3.8 cm) ring at the top, and tie it in position.

11. Dab all knots on the jute string with the hot glue and trim the ends.

12. Place a line of hot glue on the inside of the rings and fold over the fabric at the top and the bottom. Trim the fabric.

13. Install the components for the hanging lantern kit.

70

FLEECE OCTOPUS

Low-sew projects and fleece were made for each other. Turn a foam ball and some braided fringe into your new best eight-armed friend.

You Will Need:

» Sharp scissors
» Ruler or measuring tape
» Piece of fleece, 16 inches (40.6 cm) square
» 1 foam ball, 3 inches (7.6 cm) in diameter
» 12 inches (30.5 cm) of string
» 18 inches (45.7 cm) each of two different designs of ribbon, ⅜ inch (9.5 mm) wide
» Felt scraps in white, gray, and black
» Craft glue
» 12 inches (30.5 cm) of dark pink embroidery floss
» Embroidery needle
» Piece of polka-dotted quilting cotton, 8 inches (20.3 cm) square
» Sewing machine or needle and thread
» Thread

Cut the Legs

1. Cut away a roughly 5-inch (12.7 cm) square from each corner of the fleece; the cutting does not need to be exact or perfectly neat.

2. Cut six evenly spaced snips along the remaining edges. Each snip is about 5 inches (12.7 cm) in length, but again they do not need to be exact or perfectly neat (figure 1).

3. Place the ball in the center of the fleece and wrap it up, gathering all the fabric together in one spot. Use string to tie the gathered fabric tightly together, pulling the fleece taut to smooth out the wrinkles (figure 2).

4. Cut each ribbon into four lengths, each measuring 4½ inches (11.4 cm).

DESIGNER:
Abby Glassenberg

STITCH FACTOR:

low sew

>>>>>>>>>>>>>

WHAT YOU'LL DO:
Braiding &
simple sewing

figure 1

figure 2

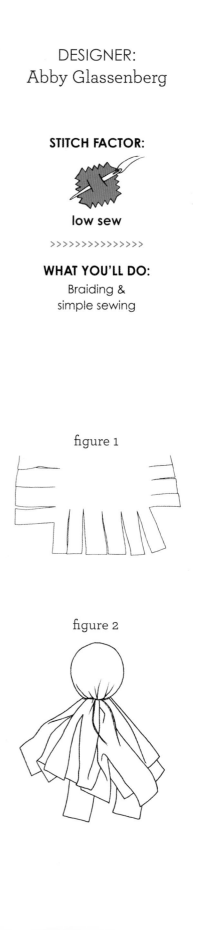

Never Been Stitched

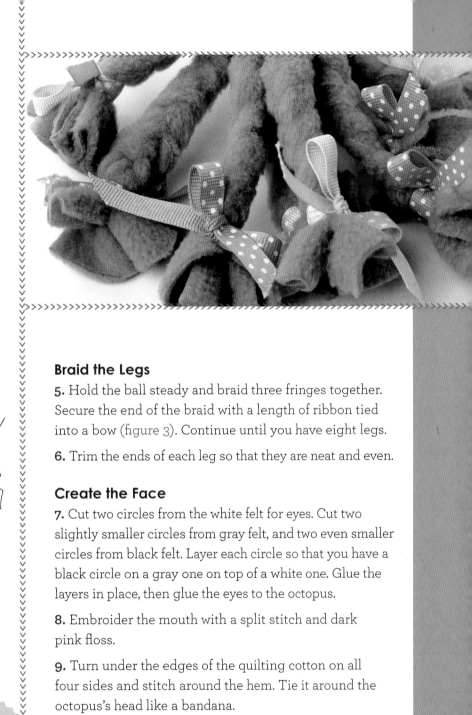

figure 3

Braid the Legs

5. Hold the ball steady and braid three fringes together. Secure the end of the braid with a length of ribbon tied into a bow (figure 3). Continue until you have eight legs.

6. Trim the ends of each leg so that they are neat and even.

Create the Face

7. Cut two circles from the white felt for eyes. Cut two slightly smaller circles from gray felt, and two even smaller circles from black felt. Layer each circle so that you have a black circle on a gray one on top of a white one. Glue the layers in place, then glue the eyes to the octopus.

8. Embroider the mouth with a split stitch and dark pink floss.

9. Turn under the edges of the quilting cotton on all four sides and stitch around the hem. Tie it around the octopus's head like a bandana.

Skip the Stitching!

Need an octopus in a hurry? Create the mouth (in step 8) with a little half circle of black felt, and leave the edges of the bandana raw.

ORIGAMI FABRIC HAT

This project is a fun twist on the traditional newspaper hat.
Scraps of fusible web and grommets hold the folds in place.

DESIGNER:
Jessica Okui

STITCH FACTOR:

no sew

>>>>>>>>>>>>>>>

WHAT YOU'LL DO:
Fusing &
grommets

figure 1

figure 2

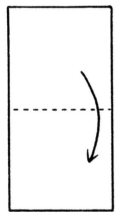

You Will Need:

» Cotton fabric of your choice, at least
  22¾ x 14 inches (57.8 x 35.6 cm)
» Scissors
» Fray retardant
» Spray starch
» Iron and ironing surface
» Paper-backed fusible web
» 2 grommets, ⁷⁄₁₆-inch (1.1 cm), plus setter
  and anvil (you can buy all this as a kit)
» Fabric pen
» Hammer

Note: *This hat is made to fit children ages
four to seven years old. For an older child cut
the fabric ½ to 1 inch (1.3 to 2.5 cm) wider. Test
out the fit with a paper version first.*

Prep the Fabric

1. Cut the fabric into a 22¾ x 14-inch (57.8 x 35.6 cm)
rectangle. Apply fray retardant to all edges of rectangle.
Let dry.

2. Spray starch on the fabric and iron it. This will help
give your hat more structure.

Fold the Hat

3. With the right side of the fabric face down, fold it in
half widthwise (figure 1). Press the fold with the iron.

Tip: *Make each fold crisp for a stronger hat.*

4. Fold the fabric in half lengthwise (figure 2). Press
with iron and unfold.

continued ⟶

Play

5. Fold both the upper left and right corners of the rectangle down to meet in the center (figure 3). Press the folds with the iron, and unfold.

6. Cut out two triangles from the paper-backed fusible web. Place the adhesive's shiny side face down on the fabric and fuse it according to the manufacturer's instructions. Let cool. Peel off the paper backing.

7. Fold both the left and right corners to meet in the center again (as you did in step 5). Iron over the triangle area to fuse the folded fabric. Fold the bottom of the hat up on the dotted line as shown in figure 4.

8. Fold the top of the rectangle down to meet the bottom edge on the dotted line shown in figure 5. Turn the hat over.

9. Follow steps 7 and 8 (figures 4 and 5) to fold the bottom of the other side of the hat.

10. Cut out a rectangular strip of iron-on web and iron it, shiny side down, onto the fabric. Let cool. Peel off the paper backing. Fold the flap down, and iron to fuse the fabric.

11. Your hat should now look like figure 6. Flip it over.

12. With the fabric pen and using the inside hole of the grommet as a template, trace two circles on each end of the fabric rectangle (figure 7). Cut out the holes through all layers of the fabric.

13. Set a grommet in each hole.

Make It Your Own

Make a hat in nautical prints for pretend play on the ocean waters or floral prints for a high-tea party. Then add pins, badges, or screenprint a child's name on the rim of the hat to personalize it.

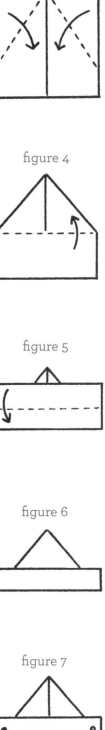

figure 3

figure 4

figure 5

figure 6

figure 7

FELT PENCIL ROLL

A scrap of felt, some well-placed cuts, and a handy tie create the perfect pencil holder, just the thing to keep your little artist organized.

Made with clever cutting!

You Will Need:

» ⅓ yard (30.5 cm) of wool or wool-blend felt*
» Ruler
» Disappearing fabric marker or tailor's chalk
» Craft knife
» Self-healing mat (optional, but helpful)
» 1 yard (.9 m) of leather cord
» 24 colored pencils

*Note: *If you are using a wool-blend felt, you can make it softer and slightly thicker by soaking it in hot water, putting it in the dryer until almost dry, and then ironing it.*

Cut the Felt

1. Cut the felt into a 9 x 33-inch (22.9 x 83.8 cm) rectangle.

2. Using a ruler and disappearing fabric marker or tailor's chalk, mark one row of 24 dashes that are ½ inch (1.3 cm) long and ½ inch (1.3 cm) apart, starting 3 inches (7.6 cm) from the long edge and 1 inch (2.5 cm) in from the short edge. Mark another row of identical dashes ½ inch (1.3 cm) away from the first (figure 1).

3. Repeat these markings 3 inches (7.6 cm) in from the other long edge and 1 inch (2.5 cm) in from the short edge: Using a ruler, mark one row of 24 dashes that are ½ inch (1.3 cm) long and ½ inch (1.3 cm) apart. Mark another row of identical dashes ½ inch (1.3 cm) away from the first.

4. Using a craft knife and self-healing mat (if desired), cut along the dashes to create slits for the pencils to slide through.

Attach the Tie

5. Attach the cord by cutting a small hole 1 inch (2.5 cm) in from and centered on the short edge. Fold the cord in half, tie a loop knot, and thread the two loose ends through the hole (figure 2).

6. Fill your roll with pencils by threading them through the cuts, roll it up, wrap the cord around, tie, and enjoy!

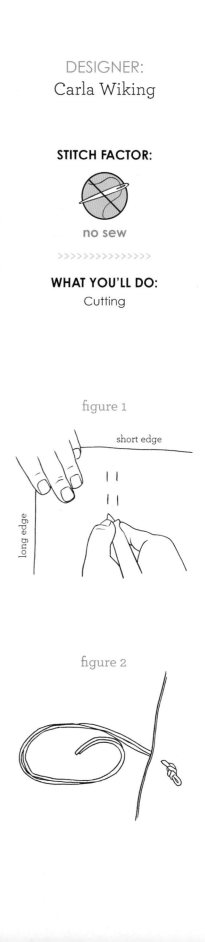

DESIGNER:
Carla Wiking

STITCH FACTOR:

no sew

>>>>>>>>>>>>>

WHAT YOU'LL DO:
Cutting

figure 1

short edge

long edge

figure 2

PUP TUTU

Strips of tulle and your favorite four-legged=fun for hours! Adjust the amounts and measurements to create a tutu for the whole fam.

You Will Need:

» 18 inches (45.7 cm) of elastic, ½ inch (1.3 cm) wide
» Straight pins
» Sewing machine or needle and thread
» 3¼ yards (3 m) of pink tulle fabric, 54 inches (137.2 cm) wide

Skip the Stitching!

Instead of stitching the elastic ends together in step 1, cut your elastic a bit longer than you need and tie them together in a knot.

DESIGNER:
Cynthia Shaffer

STITCH FACTOR:

low sew

>>>>>>>>>>>>>>

WHAT YOU'LL DO:
Knotting & simple sewing

Create the Band

1. Overlap the ends of the elastic by ½ (1.3 cm) inch, pin, and machine-stitch it in place, securing both cut ends.

Attach the Tulle

2. Cut the tulle fabric crosswise into 12 strips that measure 54 inches (137.2 cm) wide by 9 inches (22.9 cm) long.

3. Cut these strips into 17-inch (43.2 cm) lengths to yield thirty-five 17 x 9-inch (43.2 x 22.9 cm) lengths.

4. Fold one length of tulle in half lengthwise and slide it under the elastic circle (figure 1).

5. Pull the ends of the tulle around the elastic and through the folded end of the tulle strip, and pull up close to the elastic (figure 2).

6. Repeat steps 4 and 5 with the remaining 34 tulle strips, placing them side by side around the elastic.

figure 1

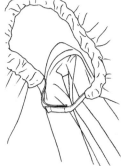

figure 2

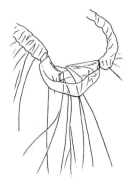

Never Been Stitched

CRAFTY KID APRON

Keep those would-be messes at bay with a sweet and simple apron. With just three sewn sides, you can easily adjust the size.

Only three seams!

You Will Need:

» Ruler or measuring tape
» Piece of fabric, 13 x 18 inches (33 x 45.7 cm)*
» Straight pins
» Fabric glue
» 1 package of double-fold bias tape, ¼ inch (6 mm) wide
» Marking tool
» Scissors
» Sewing machine
» Thread to coordinate with the fabric and ribbon
» 1¾ yards (1.6 m) of ribbon, 1½ inches (3.8 cm) wide
» Fray retardant

Note: *For the main apron body, use a vinyl without too much sheen or a fabric that doesn't fray much.*

Cut the Apron

1. Measure 5½ inches (14 cm) from the top edge of the fabric along both 18-inch (45.7 cm) edges and place a straight pin on the spot.

Add the Bias Tape

2. Starting at one of the pinned spots, glue the bias tape down the side of the apron by opening it and squeezing out a bead of glue inside the tape, working about 6 inches (15.2 cm) at a time. Use your finger and spread the glue. Place the tape on one edge of the fabric and then fold it over.

Tip: *Keep a wet paper towel on hand to clean up any glue messes.*

3. When you get to the corner, go around the corner and then fold over the excess bias tape and glue it in place. Run the bias tape all the way around the bottom edge and back up the other side to the pinned spot. Cut the bias tape.

DESIGNER:
Joan K. Morris

STITCH FACTOR:

low sew

WHAT YOU'LL DO:
Gluing &
simple sewing

figure 1

figure 2

4. Along the top edge of the apron, measure in 4½ inches (11.4 cm) from each end, and mark with a marking tool. Measure down each side 6 inches (15.2 cm). Fold over each corner at the measurements.

5. From the wrong side, machine-stitch ½ inch (1.3 cm) in from both folded edges. Cut the excess fabric off ½ inch (1.3 cm) from the stitching (figure 1).

6. Fold the top edge under ½ inch (1.3 cm) and machine-stitch it in place.

Add the Strap & Ties

7. For the neck, cut a 20 ½-inch (52.1 cm) length of the ribbon, making sure the length of the neck ribbon fits your child: It needs to slip over the child's head. Following the manufacturer's instructions, place fray retardant on both edges of the cut neck ribbon.

8. On the wrong side of the apron, place one end of the neck ribbon in position ¾ inch (1.9 cm) in from the top apron edge and pin it in place. Machine-stitch the ribbon to the fabric ½ inch (1.3 cm) from the top edge, stitching along the stitch line that is already there. To provide additional strength, stitch it again. Repeat with the other end of the neck, making sure the ribbon doesn't twist.

9. For the side ties, cut two 17-inch (43.2 cm) pieces of ribbon. Apply fray retardant to each end of both pieces.

10. On the wrong side of the apron, place one of the ribbons at the folded corner, with the edge lined up with the apron edge. Pin in place and machine-stitch ½ inch (1.3 cm) from the edge (figure 2). Fold the ribbon over itself into position and pin in place. Machine-stitch along the same line of stitches. Repeat for the other side tie.

OWL
POCKET PILLOW

This simple owly comes together with just a few stitched seams.
The surprise: a secret pocket in the back for storing messages.

DESIGNER:

Joan K. Morris

STITCH FACTOR:

low sew

>>>>>>>>>>>>>>

WHAT YOU'LL DO:
Simple sewing
& gluing

You Will Need:

» Template (page 123)
» Straight pins
» Scraps of felt in white,
  black, and blue
» Scissors
» Fabric glue
» ½ yard (45.7 cm) of fabric*
» Thread to match the fabric
» Sewing machine
» Pen or knitting needle
» Iron and ironing surface
» Hand-sewing needle
» Polyester fiberfill

*Note: *Pick a patterned fabric*
that simulates feathers.

Cut the Pattern Pieces

1. Cut out the template shapes for the owl body, the background eyes, the nose, the eyes, and the pupils.

2. Pin the background eye pattern onto the white felt and cut one out. Pin and cut out the nose and two eye pupils from the black felt. Pin and cut out two eyes from the blue felt.

3. Using the fabric glue, glue the blue eyes in place on the white-eye background felt. Spread the glue evenly on the back of each piece. Glue the black eye dots in place on the blue eyes. Glue the black nose in position on the white eye background. Let the glue dry completely.

4. Fold the body fabric in half with the wrong sides together. Pin the body pattern on the folded fabric, making sure to run the design of the fabric to look like feathers, if appropriate. Cut the body out.

Make the Pocket

5. Pin the pocket pattern on the fabric fold as indicated. Cut the pocket out.

6. With the pocket fabric folded right sides together, machine-stitch around three edges of the pocket (do not stitch the folded edge) using a ½-inch (1.3 cm) seam allowance and leaving a 2-inch (5.1 cm) opening in the bottom edge.

7. Turn the pocket right side out through the opening in the bottom edge and push out the corners with a closed pen or a knitting needle. Press the pocket flat, making sure to fold the fabric in at the opening. Hand-stitch the opening shut.

continued ⟶

85

8. Pin the pocket in position on one of the owl body pieces; this will become the back of the pillow. You can try and hide the pocket by matching the pattern of the fabric. Machine-stitch around the three edges to create the pocket (figure 1). Stitch as close as you can to the edge. Leave the folded end unstitched and open at the top.

Assemble the Owl

9. Glue the felt eyes in position on the front of the owl, making sure to spread the glue to the edge. Let the glue dry.

10. Pin the front and back of the owl together, with right sides facing and matching all edges. Machine-stitch all the way around the edge of the owl, leaving a 4-inch (10.2 cm) opening at the bottom.

11. Clip the ear points carefully above the stitching line; this will help the ears stay pointed when you turn it right side out. Clip any curves. This also helps the pillow keep its shape when turned right side out.

12. Turn the owl right side out and push out the ear corners with a pen or knitting needle. Push the seams out with your hand to get the shape right.

13. Start stuffing the pillow through the opening in the bottom. Stuff the ears first, making sure to fill them kind of tight so they hold their shape. Keep stuffing the pillow, not too tight, all the way to the bottom edge.

Tip: *If you pull the fiberfill apart and put in one small hand-ful at a time, your pillow will have a much nicer shape.*

14. Hand-stitch the bottom edge closed.

figure 1

Make It Your Own

With a few simple adjustments to the felt face pieces, you can easily turn this pocket pillow into another animal. Try making a fox or a cat!

Never Been Stitched

TEDDY BEAR BACKPACK

Is it a treasured stuffed animal or "found" fabric? Both!
Transform a favorite teddy into a handy, huggable bag.

You Will Need:

» Your favorite teddy bear
» Measuring tape
» Sharp scissors
» A nylon zipper
» Straight pins
» 2 straps*
» Clear nail polish (optional)
» Sewing needle and thread

*Note: *You can use old cloth belts, key lanyards, repurposed straps from another bag, or even ribbons as long as they are thick and sturdy enough.*

Prep the Bear

1. Select a section on the teddy bear's back that is wide enough to be an opening for the bag, and carefully cut a slit across it that's about 3 inches (7.6 cm) wide (figure 1).

2. Pull out the stuffing so that the teddy's body is empty. This part is a lot easier and neater if the teddy has separate body, arm, and leg cavities, but if it doesn't, stitch across the bear's armpits and thighs to create a separate body cavity.

Install the Zipper

3. Hold the zipper up to the slit you cut in step 1, and carefully cut it so that it becomes the same length as the slit.

4. Position the zipper inside the slit and pin it in place (figure 2).

5. Sew the zipper into place.

Add the Straps

6. Pin one end of one of the straps into place on the teddy's upper right back. Play around with the length a bit by placing the bear on your back (or whomever you're

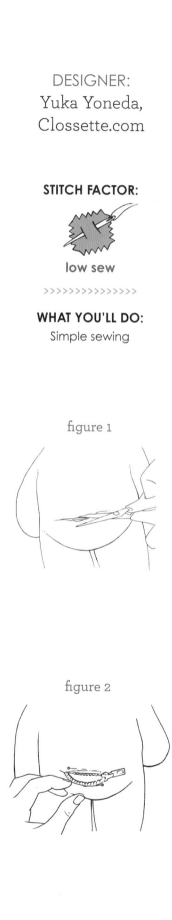

DESIGNER:
Yuka Yoneda,
Clossette.com

STITCH FACTOR:

low sew

>>>>>>>>>>>>>

WHAT YOU'LL DO:
Simple sewing

figure 1

figure 2

making this bag for) and see how long or short the strap should be; the other end should attach at the top of the leg. Once you decide on the proper length, cut your strap (remember to leave about 1 inch [2.5 cm] extra since you will need some excess strap). Cut another strap to match.

Tip: *If the material you're using for your straps has an unfinished edge and you don't want to hem it, brush it with some clear nail polish to keep it from fraying.*

7. Sew both of your straps into place at the shoulders and the tops of the legs. Alternatively, if you're using key lanyards with hooks at the end for your straps, you can cut holes in your teddy's shoulders and pass the hooks through so that you only have to sew on one side of your straps instead of both.

Make It Your Own

A teddy bear makes a lovely backpack, but what about the other stuffed animals in your collection? With just a few simple adjustments, you can use the same steps to make a dachshund duffle bag. Or a hippo hip pack.

CATERPILLOW

Give a jersey pillowcase a playful upgrade...without a single stitch!
This too-cute caterpillar is perfect for nighttime–or anytime!–snuggling.

DESIGNER:
Joan K. Morris

STITCH FACTOR:

no sew

WHAT YOU'LL DO:
Fusing & tying

You Will Need:

» 1 jersey pillowcase*
» Super-weight fusible web tape, ⅝ inch (1.6 cm) wide
» Iron and ironing surface
» Polyester fiberfill
» Bright colored string
» White glue
» Small pieces of felt in white, black, pink, yellow, orange, and turquoise
» Template (page 121)

*Note: *To create the segments of the caterpillar's body, you must use a stretchy jersey pillowcase for this project. You can make two caterpillars from one pillow.*

Prep the Pillowcase

1. Cut the pillowcase in half lengthwise, from the open hemmed side to the other short side edge.

2. Turn the pillowcase wrong side out and fuse the cut edge together using the ⅝-inch-wide (1.6 cm) fusible web tape, leaving the hemmed edge open.

Create the Face

3. To make the antennae, at each corner of the pillowcase, stuff a handful of fiberfill and make it as round as possible.

4. Cut an 18-inch (45.7 cm) piece of the string, and knot it as tightly as you can 3 inches (7.6 cm) in from the corner. Wrap the string tightly around the fabric, working up toward the stuffed corner to form a round end for the antenna. Wrap it back down to the knot and tie it to the other end. Place a dab of white glue on the knot and trim the ends of the string. Repeat for the other antenna.

5. From the white felt, cut out two circles. From the black felt, cut out two little ovals for pupils. From the pink felt, cut out a small oval shape for the nose.

6. Following the manufacturer's instructions, use the fusible web tape to fuse the black ovals to the white circles, then fuse the white circles to the pillowcase in place on the head. Fuse the pink felt nose in place under the eyes.

Stuff the Body

7. To create the head, loosen the fiberfill and then stuff the head until you get the size you want, moving it around to create a circular shape. Cut a 12-inch (30.5 cm) piece of string, and wrap it tightly around the pillowcase at the base of the head, tightening up on the head. Tie a square knot.

8. Stuff the next section of the body the same way, and tie off the string with a square knot. Repeat this until you have five total segments, making the last two a little smaller. Leave the hem at the bottom. Dab a little glue on all of your square knots and trim the ends.

Make the Feet

9. Use the caterpillar feet template to cut out 5 felt pieces in assorted colors. Tie these around the string ties between each segment, working from the top so the knot is underneath and the feet hang below.

Play

91

MONSTER TISSUE COZY

Just cut and glue!

Scare off the sniffles for good! Stitch seams along the short edges, and glue on the face elements to create a silly monster face.

DESIGNER:
Cynthia Shaffer

STITCH FACTOR:

low sew

>>>>>>>>>>>>>

WHAT YOU'LL DO:
Simple sewing
& gluing

You Will Need:

» Felt rectangle, at least
  7 x 8 inches (17.8 x 20.3 cm)
» Straight pins
» Sewing machine or needle
  and thread
» Templates (page 122)
» Orange, hot pink, and
  black felt scraps
» Index card
» Craft spray adhesive

Make the Cozy

1. Cut the felt rectangle to measure 6¼ x 7½ inches (15.9 x 19.1 cm).

2. Fold the panel in half lengthwise and mark the half-way point on both sides with pins.

3. Fold the bottom portion up and overlap the pinned halfway point by ¼ inch (0.6 cm). Pin in place.

4. Fold the top portion down and overlap the bottom portion by ¼ inch (0.6 cm). Pin in place.

5. Stitch the short side edges closed with ½-inch (1.3 cm) seam allowance.

6. Trim all four corners at an angle.

7. Turn the cozy right side out. Use a straight pin to pull the 4 corners out.

Create the Face

8. Using the templates and the scraps of felt, cut out all the parts you need to assemble the monster face.

9. Make a note of which pieces need to be adhered first, second, and so on. Keep in mind that some pieces are adhered to the bottom portion of the cozy.

10. Using an index card, mask off sections of the felt pieces that you don't want adhesive on. Spray the felt pieces and adhere them to the cozy.

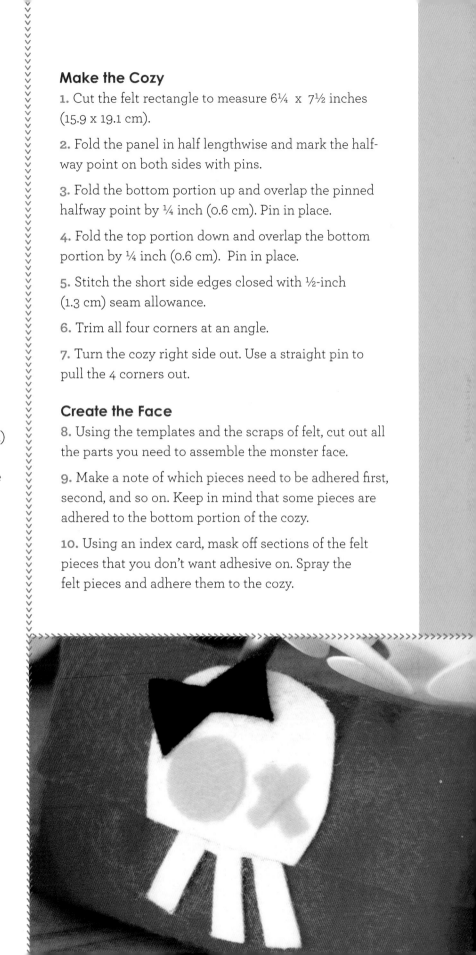

SILLY SOCK MONSTERS

What's better than sock monsters? Sock monsters that you don't have to sew. Grab some rice and some socks, and you're set to go.

DESIGNER:
Wendi Gratz

STITCH FACTOR:

no sew

>>>>>>>>>>>>>

WHAT YOU'LL DO:
Cutting & tying

figure 1

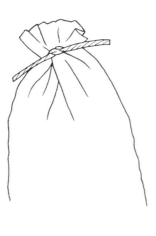

You Will Need:

» 1 sock (contrasting heel and toe colors are great for this)
» Scissors
» Yarn
» Rice
» Disappearing fabric pen
» 2 safety eyes
» Scraps of felt for reinforcing the eyes (optional)
» Polyester fiberfill for a hat (optional)

Prep the Sock

1. Cut the sock across the foot, a bit closer to the heel than to the toe. The long piece with the leg can be a large sock monster; the shorter piece with the toe can be a baby monster or a hat.

2. Starting with the larger piece, gather and tie one end of the sock with yarn (figure 1). If you do that while the sock is inside out, the finished end will be neater, but you can only do that with one end; the other end will have to be tied and closed from the outside so the gathering and tying will be visible on the finished monster. If you make that the bottom of the body, it will be hidden when you stand the monster up. If you do it at the head, you can hide it under a hat.

Add the Eyes

3. Turn the sock right side out, fill it partially with rice, and mush it down so it stretches out a bit. Mark the placement of the eyes with a disappearing fabric pen while the sock is filled.

4. Dump out the rice and insert the safety eyes following the manufacturer's instructions. If your sock is going to be played with a lot, add some felt circles behind the eyes to help keep them from popping through the knit fabric when it stretches out.

continued ⟶

5. Refill the sock with rice—all the way to the top this time. Mush it down so it stretches out a bit and add some more rice. Tie off the open end tightly with yarn. Stand your sock monster up and mush it around to play with it.

Make the Extras

6. You can turn the toe piece (from step 1) into a baby monster. Fill it with rice to mark the placement of the eyes on the contrasting toe "face." Dump the rice out, insert the safety eyes (with or without felt), and refill. Tie off the open end and play with it.

7. Or turn the toe into a hat. Stuff a bit of fiberfill into the tip of the toe and tie it off so it's a ball. It's cute, and now it looks a lot less like the toe of a sock. If your sock has a contrasting color on the toe, try to tie it off where the color changes. Stick it on your monster's head to keep him toasty warm.

8. Give your monster some knobby bits. After filling the monster with rice, pull up a rice-filled bit wherever you want a knob. Tie a knot under the knob to hold it in place. You can put knobs in a ridge down his back, give him some knobby feet, or a couple of knobby bumps on his head. You could even give him some knobby eyes.

9. Maybe you want to add a tuft of hair? Turn the sock right side out. Wind a bunch of yarn around one hand and pull it off so it's a nice, neat clump. Tuck it into the open end of the sock so that one end of the yarn loops is just peeking out the opening. Tie the opening tightly closed (figure 2). When you turn the sock right side out, that tuft of yarn will be growing out of the top of your monster's head. Cut the loops into individual hairs or leave them as loops.

figure 2

TO-A-TEE CARRYALL

Transform a T-shirt and tote everything you need in style!
The stitched edge is entirely optional.

You Will Need:

- » 1 T-shirt, size large
- » Scissors
- » Pencil or chalk
- » Ruler
- » Straight pins
- » Sewing machine
- » Coordinating sewing thread
- » Scrap of coordinating knit fabric
- » Perle cotton
- » Large-eye hand-sewing needle

Cut the T-shirt

1. Fold the T-shirt in half lengthwise. Cut the neckline and the shoulders from the folded T-shirt as shown in (figure 1). The strap should be at least 2½ inches (6.4 cm) wide. Do not throw the neck portion away; you will use it for the pocket.

2. Cut the bottom hem off the T-shirt.

3. Turn the cut T-shirt inside out and fold it in half lengthwise.

4. Make a mark 3½ inches (8.9 cm) in from the side fold and 3½ inches (8.9 cm) up from the bottom. Draw a line connecting the marks, creating a triangle. Cut across the line through all thicknesses.

5. Unfold the T-shirt, pin the bottom edges together (with right sides still facing), and machine-stitch the bag closed. Stitch again, close to the first stitching line, to add stability to this seam.

Make the Pocket

6. Using the neck portion of the cut T-shirt, create the pocket. Measure the straight top edge of the pocket, and from the coordinating fabric scrap, cut a strip that measures 2 inches (5.1 cm) by the width of the pocket at the top edge.

98

DESIGNER:
Cynthia Shaffer

STITCH FACTOR:

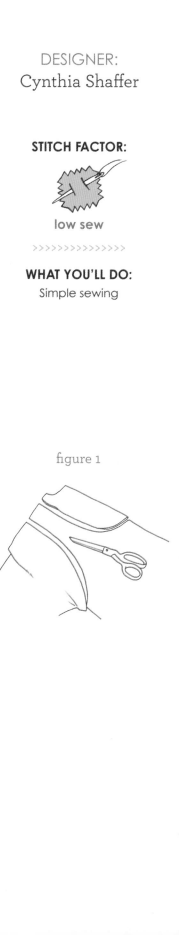

low sew

>>>>>>>>>>>>>>

WHAT YOU'LL DO:
Simple sewing

figure 1

figure 2

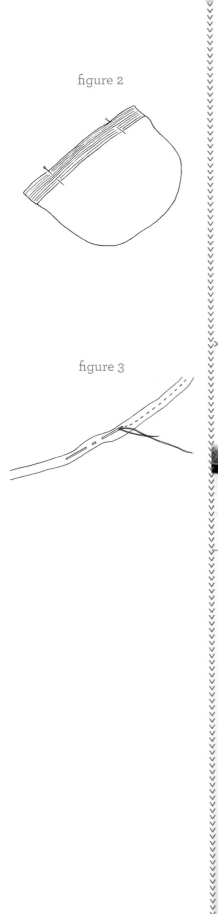

figure 2

7. Fold the strip in half with wrong sides together, and machine-stitch it to the top of the pocket, with right sides facing and raw edges matching (figure 2).

8. Pin the pocket to the front of the bag and, using the perle cotton and the large-eye hand-sewing needle, stitch the pocket in place.

Finish the Edges

9. Using the perle cotton and the large-eye hand-sewing needle, sew the edges of the tote's handle under ¼ inch (6 mm) (figure 3), using a big running stitch.

figure 3

BOARDWALK
BACKPACK

Whip this bag up quick in any color, and you're ready for the trail, the boardwalk, or wherever your travels take you.

DESIGNER:
Amanda Carestio

STITCH FACTOR:

no sew

>>>>>>>>>>>>>>

WHAT YOU'LL DO:
Grommets &
fused appliqué

figure 1

You Will Need:

» ½ yard (45.7 cm) of thin, strong fabric (in this case, a denim blend with a bit of stretch)
» Sharp scissors
» Ruler or tape measure
» Iron and ironing surface
» 10 grommets, ⅜ inch (9.5 mm) in diameter
» Craft knife (optional)
» Straight pins
» Template (page 120)
» Piece of paper-backed fusible web, 5 x 15 inches (12.7 x 38.1 cm)
» Piece of coordinating cotton fabric, 5 x 15 inches (12.7 x 38.1 cm)
» 3½ yards (3.2 m) of rope, ¼ inch (6 mm) wide

Cut the Bag

1. Fold the fabric in half with right sides together and selvages touching. Cut a piece that measures 15 x 22 inches (38.1 x 55.9 cm). At the top cut edge, measure in 1½ inches (3.8 cm) on both sides and make a mark. Place one end of your ruler at the mark and the other end at the bottom folded corner. Trace the line and cut along it. Repeat for the other side of the bag.

2. Working at the top short edge, fold the edge over 1 inch (2.5 cm) and press. Fold the edge over again 1 inch (2.5 cm) and press.

Add the Grommets

3. Set a grommet in the center of the short edge, using the scissors or a craft knife to cut a starter hole and making sure you catch all the layers (figure 1). Repeat steps 2 and 3 for the other short edge.

continued ⟶

Carry

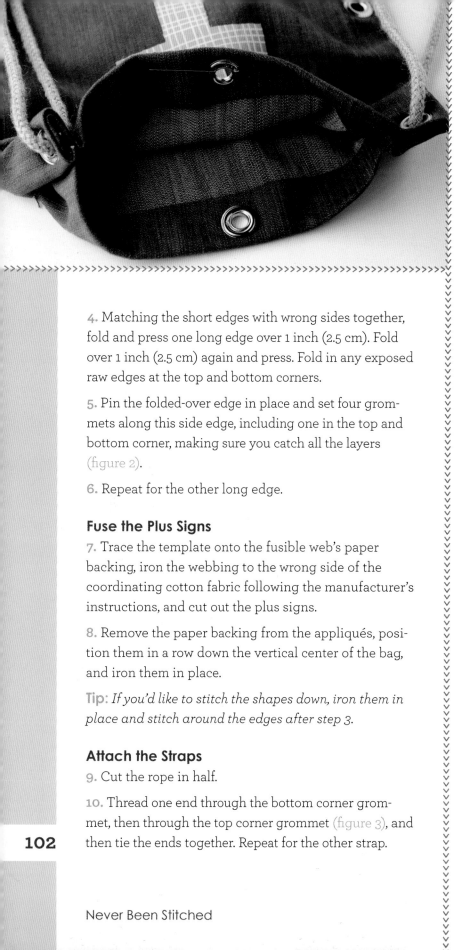

4. Matching the short edges with wrong sides together, fold and press one long edge over 1 inch (2.5 cm). Fold over 1 inch (2.5 cm) again and press. Fold in any exposed raw edges at the top and bottom corners.

5. Pin the folded-over edge in place and set four grommets along this side edge, including one in the top and bottom corner, making sure you catch all the layers (figure 2).

6. Repeat for the other long edge.

Fuse the Plus Signs

7. Trace the template onto the fusible web's paper backing, iron the webbing to the wrong side of the coordinating cotton fabric following the manufacturer's instructions, and cut out the plus signs.

8. Remove the paper backing from the appliqués, position them in a row down the vertical center of the bag, and iron them in place.

Tip: *If you'd like to stitch the shapes down, iron them in place and stitch around the edges after step 3.*

Attach the Straps

9. Cut the rope in half.

10. Thread one end through the bottom corner grommet, then through the top corner grommet (figure 3), and then tie the ends together. Repeat for the other strap.

figure 2

figure 3

102

Never Been Stitched

BANDANA BAG

This bag makes the most of fabric with pre-finished edges: the classic bandana. Just add a bit of jute webbing for the strap.

DESIGNER: Cynthia Shaffer

You Will Need:

- » Iron and ironing surface
- » 2 bandanas, 22 inches (55.9 cm) square
- » ¾ yard (68.6 cm) of blue-and-white ticking fabric
- » Ruler or tape measure
- » Straight pins
- » Sewing machine
- » Thread
- » 80 inches (203.2 cm) of 3½-inch-wide (8.9 cm) jute webbing

Cut the Panels

1. Iron the bandanas flat and using the bandana as a pattern, place one on top of the ticking fabric, with the ticking's fringed selvage edge poking out the side just ½ inch (1.3 cm). The stripes of the ticking panels should be running horizontally.

2. Cut around the bandana but do not cut the fringed selvage edge. Repeat to cut a second panel of ticking.

Create the Pocket

3. From the ticking (and with the stripes running vertically), cut a rectangle that measures 8 x 9 inches (20.3 x 22.9 cm). This will become the inside cell-phone pocket.

4. Turn under one of the pocket's short edges ½ inch (1.3 cm) and stitch in place.

5. Center the pocket on the right side of one of the ticking panels, with the hemmed pocket edge about 5 inches (12.7 cm) down from the fringy edge (figure 1).

6. Pin the pocket in place and topstitch along the sides and across the bottom.

low sew

>>>>>>>>>>>>>>

WHAT YOU'LL DO:
Simple sewing

figure 1

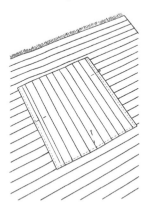

Assemble the Bag

7. Pin the bandanas together with right sides facing and stitch along three sides using a ½-inch (1.3 cm) seam allowance. Repeat for the ticking panels, leaving the fringy selvage edges for the tote opening.

8. Turn the pieces right sides out and align the bottom seam of the bandanas and the ticking panels so that the wrong sides are together.

9. Pin the top edges of the bandanas and the ticking panels together, wrong sides facing, so that the bandana is 2 inches (5.1 cm) below the top edge of the fringy selvage edge. The ticking is the lining of the tote and will be shorter than the outer bandana, but that's okay! Stitch across the top of the bandanas.

10. Fold the fringy edge of the ticking to the outside of each bandana and stitch across the top edge ½ inch (1.3 cm) from the top fold.

11. Line up the sides of the bandanas and the ticking, pin, and baste together.

Make the Strap

12. Press the length of jute webbing in half lengthwise.

13. Pin the jute wedding around the outer edges of the bandana and ticking tote (figure 2), lining up the cut edges at the lower corners.

14. Using a wide zigzag stitch, stitch the jute webbing in place starting at the bottom corner and continuing up the sides, around the strap, and then down the other side (figure 3).

15. To finish off the ends of the jute webbing, use a zigzag stitch and stitch several times back and forth along the cut edge of the jute webbing.

figure 2

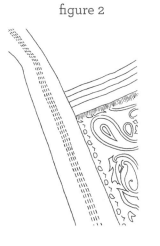

figure 3

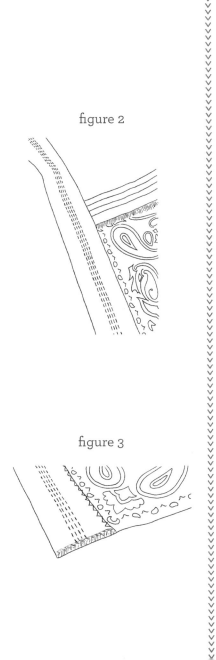

FUROSHIKI TOTE

Finish your edges or leave them raw—either way, this folded tote holds it all. Tie the handles in different ways to suit your needs.

Fold, tie, and go!

DESIGNER:
Cynthia Shaffer

STITCH FACTOR:

low sew

>>>>>>>>>>>>>

WHAT YOU'LL DO:
Simple sewing, knotting
& fused appliqué

figure 1

figure 2

Skip the Stitching!

Make this project no-sew
by using fusible hem tape
or fusible web instead of
stitching the edges.

You Will Need:

» Scissors
» Ruler or measuring tape
» 1¼ yards (1.1 m) of fabric, 42 inches (106.7 cm) wide
» Iron and ironing surface
» Sewing machine and thread (optional)
» ½ yard (45.7 cm) of fusible web
» ⅓ yard (30.5 cm) of coordinating fabric
» Glue stick or other round found object, ¾ inch (1.9 cm) in diameter
» Pencil

Create the Bag Body

1. Cut a 40-inch (101.6 cm) square from the main fabric.

2. Press the outer edges under ¼ inch (6 mm).

3. Press the outer edges under another ¼ inch (6 mm) and machine-stitch around the perimeter.

Make the Appliqués

4. Iron a piece of fusible web to the wrong side of the coordinating fabric. Leave the paper backing in place.

5. Using a found object that measures ¾ inch (1.9 cm) in diameter (like the top of a glue stick), trace circles with a pencil onto the fusible web's paper backing (figure 1).

6. Draw flower shapes freehand onto the paper-backed coordinating fabric.

7. Cut out the circles and the flowers. Remove the paper backing and stack each circle on top of the center of a flower, and then fuse them onto the hemmed square as desired (figure 2).

Tie the Handles

8. Lay the cloth out flat and tie one corner into a knot. Tie the opposite corner into a knot.

9. Grab the two remaining corners and tie them together into a square knot. Flip the two corner knots to the wrong side of the cloth.

Carry

EASY
EVERYDAY TOTE

Made with simple bound edges and a single pattern piece, this tote is the perfect home for your everyday essentials.

DESIGNER:

Joan K. Morris

STITCH FACTOR:

low sew

>>>>>>>>>>>>>

WHAT YOU'LL DO:

Simple sewing
& gluing

You Will Need:

» Template (page 122)
» Pencil
» Scrap paper for template
» Scissors
» Straight pins
» ½ yard (45.7 cm) of vinyl fabric
» Sharp scissors
» 1 package of double-fold bias tape, ¼ inch (6 mm) wide
» Fabric glue
» Sewing machine
» Thread to match the fabric
» Pen or knitting needle

Cut the Bag Shape

1. Transfer the template onto scrap paper and cut it out.

2. Pin the pattern to the fabric and cut it out.

Finish the Handles

3. Cut the double-fold bias tape 1 inch (2.5 cm) longer then the curved handle edges, one piece for each side.

4. Open the bias tape and run a line of glue along the entire inside and spread the glue with your finger.

5. With the bias tape open, place the fabric edge to the center crease and fold the other edge in place. Do this on both sides of the handles (figure 1). Let the glue dry.

Stitch the Edges

6. Fold the piece with right sides together, so you have an inside-out tote. Pin one edge in place. Using a ½-inch (1.3 cm) seam allowance, machine-stitch from the bias tape at the top to the bottom edge (figure 2). Stitch back and forth to lock the ends. Now stitch the other side edge.

7. Machine-stitch the bottom edge. You can stitch a second time to add extra strength.

8. Clip the corners. Turn the piece right side out. Push the corners out gently with a closed pen or a knitting needle.

figure 1

figure 2

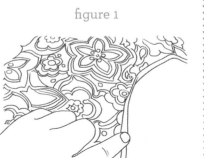

HIBISCUS GIFT TOPPER

Top your presents with these dimensional hibiscus blooms and make gift giving even sweeter.

Sweet low-sew style!

DESIGNER:
Abby Glassenberg

STITCH FACTOR:

low sew

>>>>>>>>>>>>>>

WHAT YOU'LL DO:
Gluing &
simple sewing

figure 1

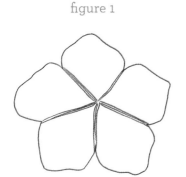

You Will Need:

» Disappearing fabric marker
» Templates (page 123)
» Piece of felt for the petals (pink, chartreuse, or cream),
  10 x 12 inches (25.4 x 30.5 cm)
» Small fabric scissors
» Piece of felt for the stamens (light or dark brown),
  10 inches (25.4 cm) square
» Piece of felt for the stem, base, and leaf (light or dark
  green), 10 inches (25.4 cm) square
» Sewing machine and/or hand-sewing needle
» Thread that matches the petals and the leaf
» Hot glue gun and glue stick
» Safety pin

Cut the Flower

1. Use a disappearing fabric marker to trace the Petal template onto felt. Cut out the petal and repeat until you have five petals.

2. Trace the Stamen template onto felt and cut it out. Repeat so that you have two stamen pieces.

3. Trace the Leaf, Base, Stem, and Pin Cover templates onto felt and cut one of each. Transfer all markings from the templates to the felt pieces.

Make the Flower

4. Stitch the first petal to the second along one side in the marked area. Attach the third petal to the second in the same way. Continue to attach petals, ending by attaching the fifth to the first (figure 1).

5. Place one stamen piece on top of the other, rotated a quarter turn to create the look of a six-pointed star. Use a dab of hot glue to stick the stamen pieces together.

continued ⟶

6. Fold the stamen pieces together, upward (figure 2), and push the glued base of the stamen through the small opening left at the bottom of the flower. Don't push it through too far, just enough that you can see it poking out of the flower.

7. Apply hot glue to the inner dotted triangle marked on the base piece and adhere it to the underside of the flower (figure 3), thereby attaching the stamen to the petals.

8. Roll up the stem piece beginning with the longer straight edge, continuing toward the curved edge. Apply hot glue along the curved edge and adhere it to secure the rolled stem.

9. Apply hot glue to the top of the rolled stem and press it to the base of the flower.

10. If desired, stitch the veins of the leaf. Apply hot glue to the bottom tip of the leaf and press it against the stem.

11. Open the safety pin and position it on the back of the leaf. Apply hot glue to the pin cover. While holding the bar of the pin against the felt with one hand, place the pin cover over the bar with the other and press to adhere the pin to the leaf.

figure 2

figure 3

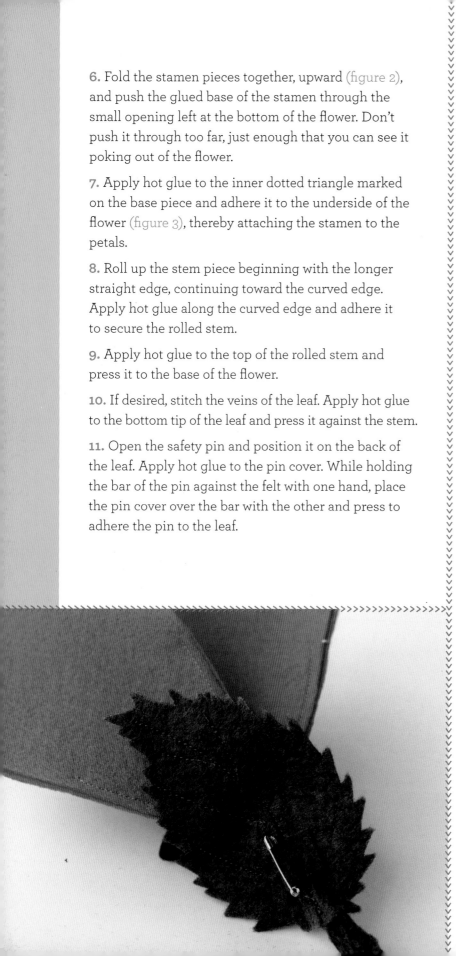

WEE FELT BOOKS

Capture inspiration, impressions, and ideas whenever they strike with these sweet notebooks.

DESIGNER: Megan Hunt

You Will Need:

» Small notebook or pocket planner to cover
» Felt for covering the book*
» Ruler
» Rotary cutter and self-healing mat
» Fabric glue
» Scissors
» Scrap of white felt, 2 x 3 inches (5.1 x 7.6 cm)
» Embroidery needle
» Black embroidery thread

Note: *You'll need an amount of felt that is twice the area of the book cover. For small books, 9 x 12-inch (22.9 x 30.5 cm) sheets from craft stores work well, but for larger ones I recommend buying yardage.*

Cut the Cover

1. First lay out the notebook on top of the felt to figure out the seam allowance you'll need to cut. Measure ½ inch (1.3 cm) on both the left- and right-hand sides of the book cover, and ¼ inch (6 mm) on the top and bottom sides (figure 1), and cut with the rotary cutter or scissors.

2. Next, measure the width of the front cover. Cut two pieces of felt that measure the same height as the first piece, and half the width of the front cover (figure 2). These two smaller rectangles of felt will serve as the inner flaps for the book cover.

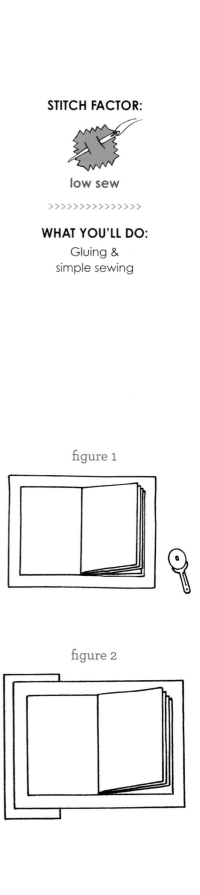

STITCH FACTOR:

low sew

>>>>>>>>>>>>>

WHAT YOU'LL DO:
Gluing &
simple sewing

figure 1

figure 2

figure 3

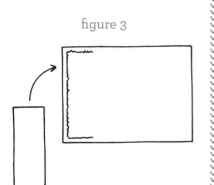

Glue the Flaps

3. Draw a thin bead of glue around the top, outside, and bottom sides of each inside cover flap cut in step 2, then carefully align each flap with the side edge of the large cover piece and press down (figure 3). Be sure to leave the inside edge of the flap unglued, because you want there to be a pocket on each side of the cover to insert the front and back cover of the notebook.

Create the Label

4. While the glue dries, you can prepare the cute label embellishment for the front cover. Use the scissors to notch the corners of the scrap of white felt to create the shape of a vintage-style label.

5. Thread the needle with a length of black embroidery thread and sew three rows of a simple running stitch on the face of the label.

6. Glue the label to the front of the felt notebook cover. When the glue dries, slide your notebook inside and take it all over town to show of your smart style and prudent note-taking abilities!

Skip the Stitching!

Create the look of the stitched label (from step 5) with a fabric marker instead.

BLOCK PRINT CARDS

With just a bit of sewing (that you could skip if you want to), these cards are inspired by bold block-print shapes.

DESIGNER:
Amanda Carestio

STITCH FACTOR:

low sew

>>>>>>>>>>>>>>>

WHAT YOU'LL DO:
Fused appliqué
& simple sewing

Skip the Stitching!

No time for stitching?
The fusible web will
hold the shapes in
place on these
cards quite well.

You Will Need:

» Pencil
» Template (page 121)
» Scrap of fusible web, 5 x 6 inches (12.7 x 15.2 cm)
» Piece of black or brown fabric, 5 x 6 inches (12.7 x 15.2 cm)
» Iron and ironing surface
» Scissors
» Plain card and envelope
» Sewing machine or needle and thread

Create the Appliqué

1. Trace the template shape onto the paper backing of the fusible web.

2. Following the manufacturer's instructions, fuse the webbing to the wrong side of the fabric and cut out the shape.

3. For the feather card, fuse the shape in place on the front of the card, stretching the shape slightly and splaying the feathers out a bit as you work.

Stitch the Card

4. Stitch down the center of the feather either by machine or by hand.

Tip: *If you're working with a needle and thread, pre-punch the holes first and then stitch a simple back-stitch down the center of the feather.*

5. For the leaf card, follow the same basic steps above, and then stitch two center lines between the leaves to create the stem.

6. Add decorative stitching to the envelope.

117

NO-SEW FLOWERS

Finally: the perfect project for your collection of scrap fabric strips! Simply gather and glue your way to a lovely flower bouquet.

No-sew a whole bouquet!

figure 1

figure 2

You Will Need:

» Scraps of fabric, approximately 2 x 16 inches
(5.1 x 40.6 cm)*

» Glue gun and glue sticks

» 12-inch (30.5 cm) wooden dowels, ³/₁₆ inch
(5 mm) in diameter, or any size desired

» Pen (optional)

» Scraps of felt

» Scissors

*Note: *No rules here—use whatever size you want.
This is the size used for this project.*

Roll the Strip

1. Bunch up the beginning of the fabric strip a bit
(figure 1); this will be the center of the flower.

2. Stick a dab of hot glue right in the center and glue
the end of the dowel to the center of the flower. Don't
worry: the tip of the dowel won't show when you're
done—unless you want it to! You can push it out more
and add something to the top of it for a cool center.

3. Run a few inches of glue along the next section of
the fabric and carefully scrunch bits of the fabric up
and press it together at the bottom of the flower. It's
like you're "ruffling" the fabric. Just keep doing this,
bit by bit. Glue, gather, stick. Repeat until you've gone
all the way around. You can use the back of a pen to
help press the glued fabric down to keep from burning
your finger.

Cover the Base

4. Finish off that base by cutting a small felt circle (any
color you'd like). It doesn't need to be a perfect circle,
just eyeball it. Cut a slit in the middle.

5. Glue and wrap the little felt circle around the base
of the flower to disguise the messy glue and fabric
(figure 2), and you're done!

119

TEMPLATES

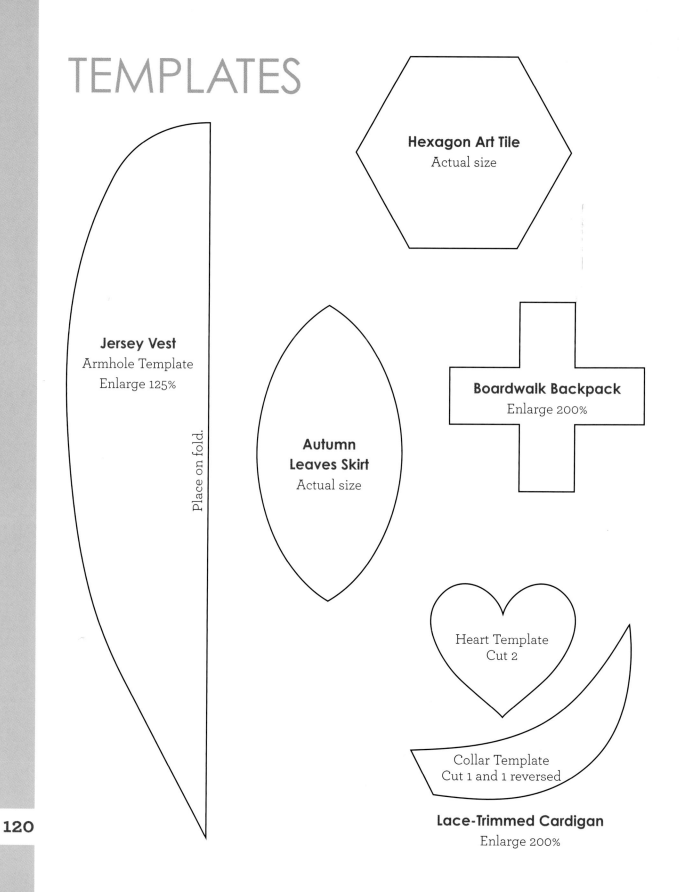

Hexagon Art Tile
Actual size

Jersey Vest
Armhole Template
Enlarge 125%

Place on fold.

**Autumn
Leaves Skirt**
Actual size

Boardwalk Backpack
Enlarge 200%

Heart Template
Cut 2

Collar Template
Cut 1 and 1 reversed

Lace-Trimmed Cardigan
Enlarge 200%

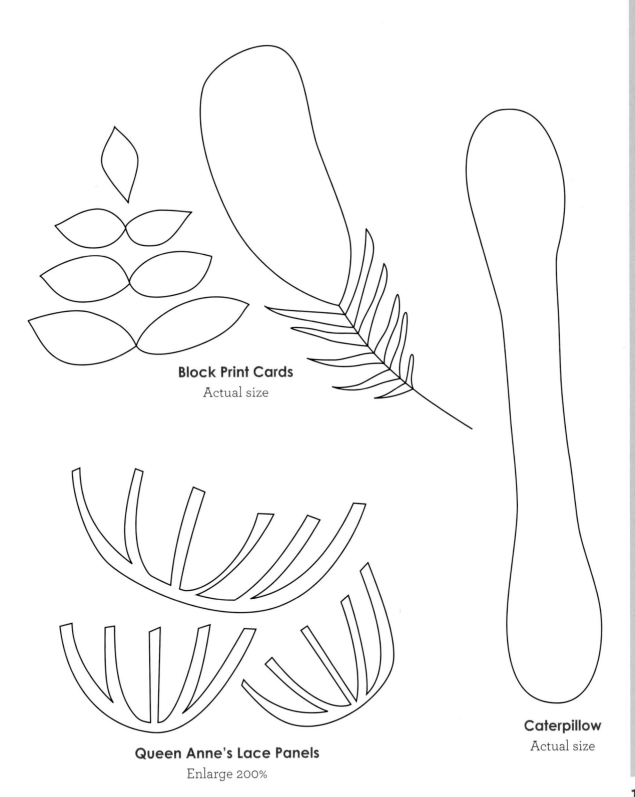

Block Print Cards
Actual size

Queen Anne's Lace Panels
Enlarge 200%

Caterpillow
Actual size

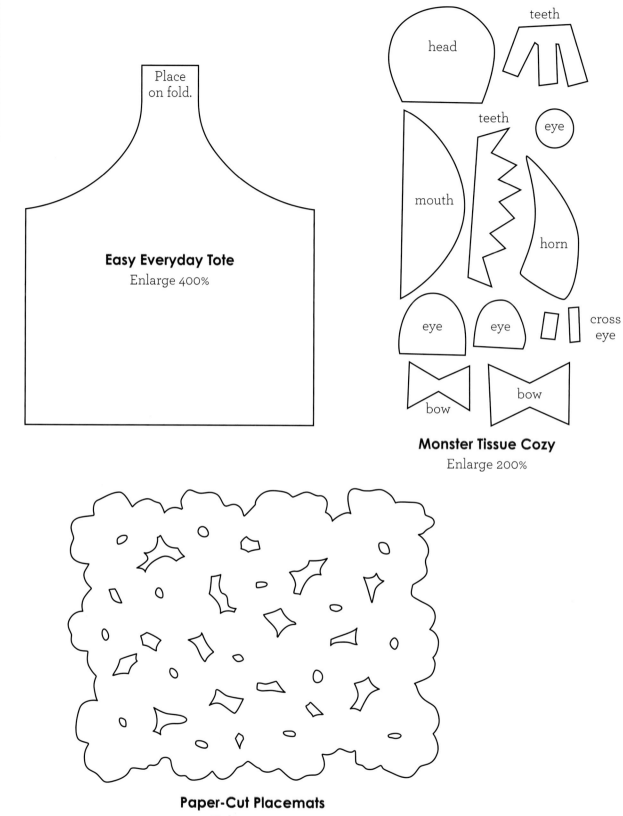

Place
on fold.

Easy Everyday Tote
Enlarge 400%

head

teeth

teeth

eye

mouth

horn

eye

eye

cross
eye

bow

bow

Monster Tissue Cozy
Enlarge 200%

Paper-Cut Placemats
Enlarge 400%

Never Been Stitched

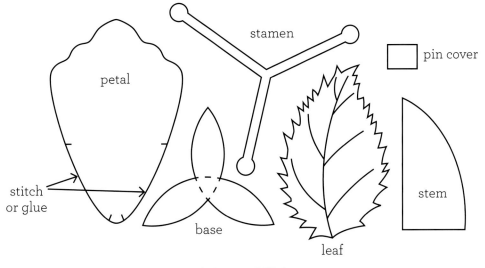

stamen

pin cover

petal

stitch or glue

base

leaf

stem

Hibiscus Gift Topper
Enlarge 200%

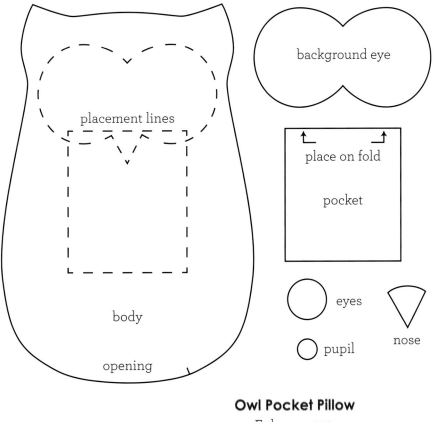

background eye

placement lines

place on fold

pocket

eyes

pupil

nose

body

opening

Owl Pocket Pillow
Enlarge 400%

123

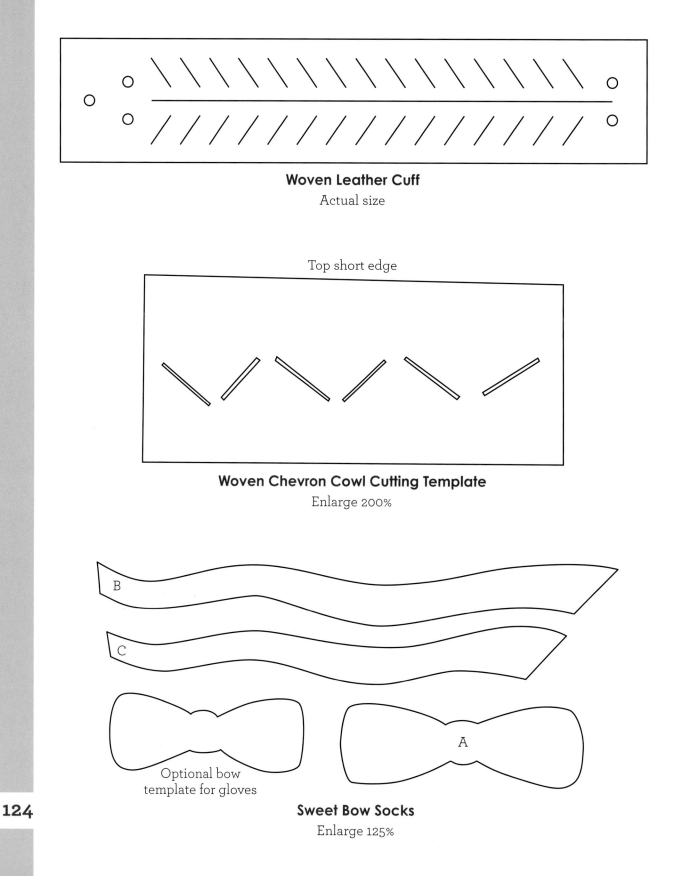

Woven Leather Cuff

Actual size

Top short edge

Woven Chevron Cowl Cutting Template

Enlarge 200%

B

C

Optional bow
template for gloves

A

Sweet Bow Socks

Enlarge 125%

Never Been Stitched

ABOUT THE DESIGNERS

Jenny Bartoy

Jenny Bartoy is the mama of two curious boys, a former project manager and film-maker, and, most recently, a designer of fabric art and handmade items that she sells in her shop on Etsy (www.jennybartoy.etsy.com). Inspired by nature, patchwork, and clean design, she loves to work with natural fibers and modern fabrics. With her dear friend Angel, she co-writes Stumbles & Stitches, a blog where they share their handmade and creative endeavors with each other and the world (www.stumblesandstitches.blogspot. com). Jenny lives in beautiful Seattle, Washington, with her archaeologist husband, their sons, and one rambunctious kitty.

Jessica Fediw

Jessica Fediw is a mom to two precious little girls and wife to a Coastie. She began her adventures in crafting after the birth of her first daughter. Many years later, the military has taken the family all over the world, but Jessica is able to craft wherever they might be. Some of those crafts include sewing, crocheting, painting, and anything else she can try out. She writes about her craft endeavors on her blog Happy Together (www.happytogethercreates.com) and shares many DIY projects there. She also has patterns and handmade items in her Etsy shop, www.ohsohappytogether.etsy.com.

Abby Glassenberg

Abby Glassenberg creates unique patterns for stuffed animals from her home studio in Wellesley, Massachusetts. Since 2005 she has shared her creations and her ideas on design, technique, and the online culture of craft through her blog (www.whileshenaps. typepad.com). Abby has a master's degree in education from Harvard and taught middle school social studies in Mississippi and Massachusetts before becoming a textile artist and the mother of three girls. Today Abby enjoys teaching people to sew and opening their eyes to the joy of designing their own stuffed animals. Abby's first book, *The Artful Bird: Feathered Friends to Make and Sew*, was an ALA Booklist top-ten craft book of 2011. Her new book, *Stuffed Animals*, about soft toy design was released in May 2013 by Lark Books. Abby has also licensed toy designs to Simplicity. You can find more of Abby's stuffed animal patterns in her Craftsy pattern shop (www.craftsy.com/user/pattern/store/330178) and her Etsy shop (www. whileshenaps.etsy.com).

Wendi Gratz

Wendi Gratz lives online at www.shinyhappy-world.com. She designs sewing, embroidery, and quilting patterns especially for beginners, and all her patterns link to free online videos teaching you every skill you'll need to complete the project. She's been playing with fabric and yarn for as long as she can remember and loves luring people into the happy needlework world. Put a needle in her hand and a sweet treat at her side and she'll be content for hours.

Megan Hunt

Megan Hunt is a project designer, blogger, and serial entrepreneur. Founder of the businesses Princess Lasertron (princesslasertron. com) and Hello Holiday (hello-holiday.com), she injects her personal brand of handcrafted design, business prowess, and sense of humor into all of her exciting pursuits and adventures. Megan loves to write, talk, and eat with friends, and she's passionate about working to support and develop entrepreneurs, and to encourage women who want to follow their passions and take risks.

Beki Lambert

Beki Lambert lives with her husband and four children in south Louisiana. She inherited her love of sewing from her mother and grandmother. She enjoys creating bags, purses, quilts, and her own line of sewing patterns. Although she put crafting on hold during her early years as a mother, Beki is back at it, thanks in part to the discovery of craft blogs. The daily feedback and sharing of ideas through blogging keeps her inspired. Beki has contributed to the Pretty Little series from Lark Books; *Craft Hope: Handmade Gifts for a Cause* (Lark Books, 2010); and Stitch magazine. Visit her online at www.artsycraftybabe.com.

Teresa Mairal Barreu

Born and raised in Spain, Teresa Mairal Barreu learned knitting, crochet, and embroidery from her sewing, knitting, lace-making mother. After moving to Australia as an adult, and after a long craft-less spell, she caught the crafting bug again, becoming interested in patchwork and fabric. She says, "Crafting keeps me sane. I love spending my spare time sewing and designing. I have more crafting projects in my head than I'll ever have time to put into practice." When not sewing, Teresa can be found drawing, painting, embroidering, or felting.

Suzie Millions

Suzie Millions is a cat-loving, vintage-dress-wearing artist and compulsive crafter. She and her musician/letterpress-printer husband, Lance Wille, live in a swinging '50s house in scenic Asheville, North Carolina. Her craft opus, *The Complete Book of Retro Crafts*, was published by Lark Books in 2008. She's also a frequent contributor to other Lark books. Her Felty Family Portraits project is featured on Martha Stewart's Living blog. She and her studio are profiled in *Where Women Create: Book of Inspiration* (Lark Books, 2010). Her artwork has been shown in galleries across the United States and in France. She dreams of moving to Holland. Visit her website: www.suziemillions.com.

Joan K. Morris

Joan K. Morris's artistic endeavors have led her down many successful creative paths, including costume design for motion pictures and ceramics. Joan has contributed projects for over 40 Lark Crafts books, including the Pretty Little series, *A is for Aprons*, several Craft Challenge books, *Leather Jewelry*, and many more over the past 10 years.

Ginger Nolker

Ginger Nolker, a teacher by profession, is a mom of three currently staying home with her little blessings. She loves creating projects that are fun and practical for her children, and that make her house a home. When she's not planning homeschooling lessons or creating something, you can find her curled up with a good book, out running, or cheering for the Packers. She and her husband, Brent, have called South Carolina home since 2009, though they are Missourians at heart. Ginger tries to enjoy each day's blessings to the fullest. Read more at thepracticalperfeccionista.wordpress.com.

Jessica Okui

Jessica Okui resides in the Bay Area of California with her husband and two children. She graduated with a graphic design degree. As a craft designer, she shares her passion for crafts on the blog Zakka Life (www.zakkalife.blogspot.com). You can also find her work in Parents magazine, Family Fun magazine, and the book *Hand in Hand* (Lark Books, 2012), to name just a few.

Cynthia Shaffer

Cynthia Shaffer is a quilter and creative sewer whose love of fabric can be traced back to childhood. At the age of six, she learned to sew and in no time was designing and sewing clothing for herself and others. After earning a degree in textiles from California State University, Long Beach, Cynthia worked for 10 years as the owner of a company that specialized in the design and manufacture of sportswear. In her spare time, Cynthia knits, paints, and dabbles in mixed-media art. Numerous books and magazines have featured Cynthia's art and photography work: she is the author of *Stash Happy: Patchwork* (Lark Books, 2011) and *Stash Happy: Appliqué* (Lark Books, 2012). She lives with her husband Scott, sons Corry and Cameron, and beloved dog Harper in Southern California. For more information visit her online at www.cynthiashaffer.com or cynthiashaffer.typepad.com.

Carla Wiking

Carla Wiking is the modern homemaker behind the popular blog small + friendly (www.smallfriendly.com). She is an eco-conscious, crafty, cooking, DIY mama who is always adding to her list of projects. A lifelong maker, she is passionate about sharing the joys of creating things by hand. Carla has never met a craft she didn't like, although her favorite creations are simple, useful, and made of natural or recycled materials. When she's not making something, she is busy creating memories with her husband and young son.

Dana Willard

Dana Willard is the author of the book, *The Fabric Selector: The Essential Guide to Working with Fabrics, Trimmings, and Notions*, and she authors the popular DIY sewing blog MADE (www.dana-made-it.com). Her eye-catching photography and easy-to-follow tutorials with fresh sewing patterns and techniques have attracted many followers. Dana's designs have been featured in various sewing books, publications, and online communities. She lives in the hot city of Austin, Texas, with her husband and three kids.

Yuka Yoneda

Yuka Yoneda is a writer, cheese lover, and JeDIY master whose love of recycled fashion led her to start Clossette.com as a resource for folks looking to revamp what they already have in their closets. Her love of crafting has a lot to do with what she's seen in New York City, where she was born and raised. She believes that if you can make it there, you can make it anywhere, so that's exactly what she does! Yuka is also the New York editor of Inhabitat.com, and her refashioned clothing and accessory ideas have been featured on Today and in Glamour and other magazines and websites. Head to Clossette.com for more of Yuka's DIY fashion ideas.

ABOUT THE AUTHOR

Amanda Carestio

Amanda's latest crafting obsessions include anything mid-century modern, making things for her new baby (she's on quilt number three currently!), and the fabulousness that is fusible web. When she's not bent over her sewing machine, editing a craft book, or exploring the Blue Ridge Mountains, Amanda enjoys spending quality time with her hubby, her sweet, sweet little girl, Miss Ruby, and her little brindle shadow, Violet. Amanda is the author of *Fa La La La Felt*, *Stash Happy: Felt*, and co-author of *Heart-Felt Holidays*. Her designs appear in several Lark Books; she blogs online at www.larkcrafts.com and at www.digsandbean.blogspot.com.

ACKNOWLEDGMENTS

No amount of stitching could have held this book together without the creativity, energy, and skills of the designers included in this book! Thank you for sharing your ingenious projects with the world.

Thanks to Thom O'Hearn for the idea. Thanks to Shannon Yokeley for her lovely design work, to Orrin Lundgren for his helpful illustrations, to Shannon Quinn-Tucker for her expert project herding, and to Kathy Brock and Valerie Shrader for their skillful edits and keen eyes.

Thanks to Cynthia Shaffer for her fabulous photography; she really made these projects sing! Thanks also to Lynne Harty for pinch hitting. Thanks to the beauteous models who appear on these pages and to the Martins for sharing their lovely home with us.

INDEX